The Late-Start
Investor

JOHN F. WASIK

The Late-Start
Investor

**The Better-Late-Than-Never Guide
to Realizing Your Retirement Dreams**

AN OWL BOOK

Henry Holt & Company ▪ New York

Henry Holt and Company, Inc.
Publishers since 1866
115 West 18th Street
New York, New York 10011

Henry Holt® is a registered trademark of Henry Holt and Company, Inc.

Library of Congress Cataloging-in-Publication Data
Wasik, John F.
    The late-start investor : the better-late-than-never guide to
realizing your retirement dreams / John F. Wasik.
        p.   cm.
    ISBN 0-8050-5502-9 (pbk.   : alk. paper)
    1. Baby boom generation—Finance, Personal.   2. Retirement income—
United States—Planning.   3. Investments—United States.
    I. Title.
HG179.W3193   1999
332.024'01—dc21   98-17435

Henry Holt books are available for special promotions and premiums.
For details contact: Director, Special Markets.

First Edition 1998

Designed by Jessica Shatan

Printed in the United States of America
All first editions are printed on acid-free paper. ∞

10   9   8   7   6   5   4

To Sarah Virginia, my morning star

CONTENTS

PREFACE

"Time is like a meteorite, a precious thing from heaven that will never return from whence it came. So once it falls to earth it's best to appreciate its journey."

Okay, so you got this far and survived without eating an apple a day or flossing or saving for a rainy day. It hasn't been an easy path, but you often find yourself thinking that an easier life would be nice. More money would do the trick, not to mention more time. How about a different house, job, or outlook? How do you do it? How do you get to that unexplored dreamland of wealth and time to enjoy it? Plunge what little you have into an exotic commodity where you stand to lose more than you invest? Play the lottery religiously and chant in front of pagan idols? Wait for Ed McMahon and Dick Clark to call?

Well, I have a really dull answer. This may come as no surprise to you, but basic saving and investing will get you where you want to be. Actually, acquiring and growing money is the easy part. It's just a numbers game that works over time in a consistent way for millions of people. There are many ways you can achieve your retirement dreams in a low-risk and high-return manner.

The more elusive part of the equation is what you want to do with that money. Money is an instrument of acquisition and change. It allows you to buy things such as financial security, houses, cars, and appliances, as well as to change your life somewhat, but it's no substitute for a life plan. It's pointless to go about investing for the future if you don't know what you want that future to look like. What's your vision? What do you need to make it real? This book will be your guide to divining the answers to those questions and giving you the financial vehicles you need to transport yourself to that new world.

Some Famous Late Starters

Since you are late to the game, the most encouraging news is that late bloomers produce the most abundant gardens. Some of the most famous late starters in history include Leo Tolstoy, Henry Ford, Alex Haley, Sam Walton, Ray Kroc (the founder of McDonald's), Ian Fleming, John Glenn, Mother Teresa, Harry Truman, and Abraham Lincoln.

They all had one thing in common: Their successes came well into their fifth decades after a long and often agonizing string of failures. In spite of the obstacles they faced, each person kept on pursuing what he or she wanted. Because they persisted, they each transformed not only their own lives but history as well. Age is no hindrance when you make up your mind to do something.

The Death of Conventional Retirement

Financial security and retirement are not the two peas in the pod they used to be. The once-conventional retirement that followed thirty or more years of employment—getting the gold watch and walking onto a tropical golf course—is a rarity in our times. Longer life spans, corporate downsizings, home-based businesses, partial retirements, employee buyouts, permanent singlehood, and later marriage and child-rearing have all worked to wipe out the conventional retirement wisdom.

Instead of absorbing an obsolete view of retirement, we should consider what I call your New Prosperity. This includes a flexible life plan that provides for your financial, vocational, physical, emotional, and spiritual needs. Unless you look at your future holistically, merely saving up a pile of money will be a meaningless act. What you are striving for is what philosopher-poet Henry David Thoreau called the "winged life." In the conclusion of *Walden,* Thoreau recounts the tale of a beautiful insect that emerges from the kitchen table after some sixty years:

> Who knows what beautiful and winged life, whose egg has been buried for ages under the many concentric layers of woodenness in the dead dry life of society, deposited at first in the alburnum of the green and living tree, which has been gradually converted into the semblance of its well-seasoned tomb,—heard perchance gnawing out now for years by the astonished family of man, as they sat round the festive board,—may unexpectedly come forth from amidst society's most trivial and handselled furniture, to enjoy its perfect summer at last![1]

There is a "perfect summer" or two awaiting you if you choose to think about what's really important to you. This book will show you how to do it with grace, style, prosperity, and vitality. It's never too late.

The Late-Start Investor

CHAPTER 1

The Truth About Retirement, Social Security, and Pensions

The Good, the Bad, and the Ugly and What You Can Do About Them

"Life invests itself with inevitable conditions, which the unwise seek to dodge, which one and another brags that he does not know; that they do not touch him;—but the brag is on his lips, the condition is in his soul."
—Ralph Waldo Emerson

We often define prosperity by what others endured in order to provide it for us. A person who created prosperity for my family was my grandmother Elizabeth. I have only an abbreviated version of her life. What I do know makes me realize how much she and other of my forebears accomplished to root my family in fertile soil long before I came on the scene.

Elizabeth's beloved father died when she was very young, so she grew up fast on a farm outside Warsaw. My ancestors were peasant farmers trying to scratch out a subsistence in a country whose borders changed with each war. At one time Poland didn't even exist in the geography of Eastern Europe; the empires of Russia and Prussia had annexed parts of it. My grandmother left Poland because after her father died from blood poisoning as a result of a cut that got infected, her mother remarried and her stepfather disliked her. She was put on the first boat to America around the turn of the century, not to seek her fortune, but to pursue her vocation. When she arrived in America, she had been accepted to a convent in New Jersey to become a bride of Christ, but her stepfather back in Poland wouldn't support that plan. As far as he was concerned, she was in America to make *money* and send it back. Being the obedient stepdaughter, Elizabeth never took her vows. Instead, she came to Chicago.

In Chicago Heights, an industrial suburb south of Chicago, she met Stanley Wasik, a proud man from a large family that emigrated to the United States from the Galicia region of Poland. Stanley got a job in a steel mill as a "chemist" and occupied his evenings after work spending his paycheck at the local saloon. An embittered alcoholic, he beat his wife as his three children watched. The marriage did not last too long: at the height of the Great Depression, Elizabeth, a beautiful and strong-willed woman, divorced Stanley.

In Elizabeth's time and strict Polish Catholic community, however, a woman was better off enduring a mate's abuse than divorcing. Instead of accepting that Stanley was an alcoholic, his family ostracized Elizabeth, taunting her and calling her a whore as she climbed the steps to church. Because she divorced, the church excommunicated her and forbade her from taking communion. For a woman who attended mass every morning, prayed every night, and hung an oversized picture of Jesus with a bleeding heart in her living room, this must have been devastating, but Elizabeth carried on. She worked hard operating a crane in a steel mill. During World War II, she labored in a munitions plant in Joliet. Then she held a position in a machine shop until she retired, which she did out of necessity, her mind frayed to the point where she had trouble finding her way home.

Along the way, Elizabeth briefly ran a grocery store and saved enough money to buy several plots of land in a suburb of Chicago. She had her son-in-law build a small house for her, where she held family gatherings and grew tomatoes in the summer. I can still smell the sausage and sauerkraut she was almost always cooking. She used the parts of animals that were typically thrown out, the ones you couldn't bear to look at if they weren't in a stew pot. She wasted little and saved a lot.

Elizabeth was truly an enigma in my life. She spoke broken English and tried to teach my three brothers and me Polish, which didn't go over too well. I never quite understood her devotion to the church even after she was excommunicated. In spite of her status in the eyes of the Catholic Church, Elizabeth raised the money to buy a stained-glass window in the local church, which she dedicated to her parents, Sebastian and Eva (only to have the church misspell her maiden name on the plaque below the window). She also went to the early mass every morning. Adding to the mystery in my eyes was that she claimed not to know her real birthday, saying that the records containing that information were lost in the war. My aunt Alice maintains that Elizabeth pretended not to know her birthday because she was constantly making one up to fool employers. She arbitrarily established Thanksgiving Day as her birthday. We also knew almost nothing about her family in Europe, only that she had a brother in the Ukraine whose letters were censored by the Soviets and a sister who had lived in France, worked for the Underground, and after being liberated from a concentration camp, committed suicide.

Elizabeth didn't share many of her secrets, but she did let us know that she had quite a coin collection. She had collected silver coins from the Depression. These were not special coins, but ordinary quarters and half-dollars. Back then, coins were minted in pure silver, so they have a greater value than today's nickel-silver alloy coins. She kept them in coffee cans in her basement. It always puzzled me why someone would bother saving seemingly ordinary coins whose value was far less than stocks or bonds held over the same period. And to keep them in coffee cans like they were nuts or washers? What was the point of that?

It took me almost twenty years to come to the conclusion that those coins were not my grandmother's legacy, but were merely symbolic of it. She had to work ten times harder than many people of her period, never mastering English, lying about her age, separated from the institution she devoted her soul to, and working in dirty, dangerous machine shops. Nevertheless, she saved enough to feed and clothe her three children as a single mother, while buying land and building her own house. All this on jobs that paid less than ten dollars an hour.

Despite hardships, Elizabeth had found a form of prosperity borne of frugality and necessity. This kind of prosperity is a spiritual legacy that outlasts estates, stocks, and bonds and influences generations to come. Elizabeth embodied a graceful way of doing more with less that transcends material or educational shortcomings.

A few years ago, my father unearthed a wedding picture of Elizabeth and Stanley. It's one of those cheap colorized jobs with a fake ballroom setting as the backdrop. Elizabeth had a confident half-smile on her face, as if she were looking into the future and telling us, "I was saving more than a smile for you."

So my first memories of money were of a coffee can filled with silver coins—a receptacle filled with hope and the promise of prosperity. If you do nothing with this book, ponder this image: Millions of uneducated people came (and still come) to America with little in their pockets, lacking an education or the right friends, much less the right language. But they succeeded and found a new prosperity. Whatever your situation, you can, too.

So You Think You're Running out of Time?

Many who haven't met their savings or investment goals are anxious about the second half of their lives, hoping they'll have enough to provide them with comfort in their older years. If you're one of these people, don't think you are alone or that it's too late to ease your fears. When the clock struck midnight on January 1, 1997, every seven seconds baby boomers born in 1946 started turning 50. Most of this first wave of 77 million people facing their sixth decade, however, are dreading the future. According to a Merrill Lynch survey, most of them have less than $3,000 saved for their retirement. With age 65 only fifteen years away, they're late-start investors; sometimes they're desperate investors.

In addition to the ticking time bomb of baby boomers unprepared for retirement, there are those who haven't saved anything at all, according to the Merrill Lynch poll. In a survey conducted recently, the most popular response as to the amount being saved for employees 45 to 64 was *zero,* according to the Employers Council on Flexible Compensation. All told, the average amount saved was a measly $720 per year.

So some of us are scratching our heads. What happened? Did the generation of the space race, the Beatles, disco, and conspicuous consumption blow their wad having a good time? Or did we simply not listen to our parents, those children of the Depression who saved every penny and are now enjoying fat pensions and a full complement of Social Security benefits? I'm sure thoughts like this have crossed your mind once or twice. Don't worry, my aim is to not reinforce your frustration, but to show you how to remedy the situation.

First, let's take a little inventory of your worst fears. Most late starters are afraid that by the time they pass 40 it's too late to do any meaningful investing and they can't invest enough to retire on without taking extraordinary risks. The numbers, however, are much more encouraging than you might think. A 40-year-old can become a millionaire by age 65 if he/she puts aside monthly investments of $594 at a modest annual return of only 12%. That sounds like a big monthly contribution, but it's easily accomplished thanks to 401(k)s, 403(b)s, and several new reforms in small-business pension plans. We'll cover how best to employ these and every other late-start option in this book.

Retirement Myths and the New Prosperity

This book is about acquiring whatever you need to achieve your own personally defined New Prosperity, but first we need to take a comprehensive look at what defined the *old* prosperity—that is, work life, pensions, and Social Security. There are many myths about each of these. You may even believe some of them yourself, and these beliefs may stand in your way as you plan for the future. So let's examine what's commonly thought about retirement in the United States and what's actually true about it.

Just about the only thing certain about the future is that aging, retirement, retirement income, and health care will *not* be the same for you as it was for your parents. People in your generation will be able to have two, maybe three lives *after* they leave their conventional work lives. Here are some of the more common misconceptions about the future:

- **Longer life means a more diverse life.** As much as some would have us boil our lives down to fun things to do with less money, it just doesn't seem to work that way for most of us. We may be taking care of our kids and parents a lot longer than we ever thought. And then there's the prospect of living thirty or more years beyond a conventional retirement age. Most likely, we'll have the opportunity to educate, reeducate, volunteer, parent, grandparent, great-grandparent, and reinvent ourselves again and again in one lifetime. Getting a late start is irrelevant unless you're in a race. What's your hurry? There's time to learn, change, and invest because we no longer work in one factory or on one farm all of our lives. Complexity brings a rich number of desserts to us at life's table.

- **Starting late doesn't mean never starting.** Sorry for the double negative here, but getting into investing for retirement late used to mean poverty in old age. We're in a new age, however. People are getting college degrees or starting new careers and businesses well into middle age and even when they are (or used to be) considered elderly. That's why getting a late start to investing is not the drawback it used to be thirty years ago. Because there are more ways to educate ourselves, more retirement vehicles, and more health-care options, aging today presents more opportunities than limitations. If you can learn about where and how to invest your money—and can stay motivated—you can save enough money for the life you want.

- **It's no longer a given that you'll be infirm and disabled when you are older.** Let's itemize some of the lifesaving advances that didn't exist before World War II: heart bypasses, hypertension medication, paramedics, artificial joints, laser surgery, no-fat foods, and hundreds of cancer treatments. There's no doubt that you'll need health care when you're older and that Medicare will be around in some form. Because of better diets, exercise, and better medical technology, though, you'll likely have a longer life in which to enjoy the money you invest. There's a reason that the fastest-growing age group in our population today is 100-year-olds, according to the U.S. Census Bureau.

- **Government support for retired persons will only get stronger.** This is perhaps one of the few items that hold true for both you and your parents. As people get older, their families also get older and they have more time for themselves. They also save more and get more involved in the community and the nation's political workings. The pre–World War II generation raised families, bought homes, saved nest eggs. Along the way they told Washington to bolster Medicare and Social Security. Why does anyone in Washington think that the 77-million-strong baby boom generation will want *less* from these programs after they worked so hard to make retirement a pleasant, more financially secure experience? If anything, given the selfishness traditionally ascribed to the me generation, they will want *more* out of retirement programs, not less. And as this generation gains power in politics, you will see a huge decrease in the political ill will toward big government programs. The anti-government sentiment just doesn't wash with those who stand to benefit the most from government benefits.

- **Pension coverage will get better, not worse.** Some 60% of Americans don't have a pension plan, according to the U.S. Department of Labor. That will change in coming years as investors discover the many plans they can set up themselves through a bank, broker, or mutual fund firm that offer some of the advantages of big-company plans. This trend alone favors late starters, especially those who are self-employed or working for small companies. Anyone can set up a pension plan. All it takes is a little knowledge and planning.

TRENDS AND PROJECTIONS OF LIFE EXPECTANCY AT AGE 65, 1940–2060

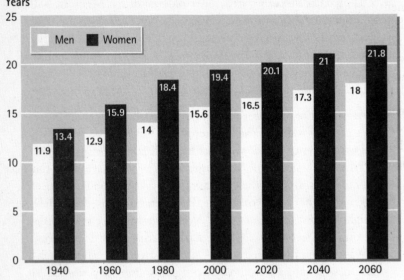

NOTE: Projections for 2000–2060 are based on the trustees' intermediate actuarial assumptions.

SOURCE: 1996 Annual Report of the Board of Trustees of the Federal Old Age and Survivors Insurance and Disability Insurance Trust Funds.

Being Honest About Starting Late: The Facts

There's no need to be in denial if your investments aren't what experts claim they should be. If you had started earlier you would have had a lot more money saved up, taken full advantage of an unprecedented run-up in the stock market (since 1982, with just two pauses), and entered your middle age with a hefty dose of financial self-confidence. You might be surprised to learn, however, that relatively few people invested in the stock market during its most torrid growth years and most of us are just poking along trying to pay the bills and are barely thinking about retirement funding. Only 21% of households headed by 35- to 44-year-olds have stocks or mutual funds—with an average value of only $4,600, reports the U.S. Census Bureau.

The reality is, few people really plan ahead or invest when it's a great time to invest. Americans within shouting distance of retirement (aged 55 plus) began saving for retirement at a median age (half above, half below) of 42. Each generation tends to live, work, and raise a family first and pay for retirement later. True, nothing will make up for lost time when it comes to investing. But there's no point in ruing what you've never had.

In the previous section, we looked at a few myths about retirement that are being punctured by modern life and developments. Now let's examine a few realities of late-start investing, how many choose to perceive them, and how we can view them in another light:

- **Starting late means taking more responsibility.** Defined-benefit pensions, those that pay a fixed monthly benefit upon retirement, used to be a staple of industrial America. In 1975, some 87% of American workers were covered by such pensions, according to the Employee Benefit Research Institute (EBRI). By 1993, however, less than 50% of the full-time workforce had defined-benefit coverage. Now more than half of all employers offer a defined-contribution plan, in which employees are given the responsibility for choosing how much money to save and how to allocate it among several mutual funds. More responsibility also means more control and better returns. Instead of accepting the mediocre-to-poor returns of large pension funds, you can invest in aggressive growth-stock funds while controlling for risk. Look at it another way: longer life expectancy means you'll have more time to learn what you need to know. In 1940, the life expectancy at age 65 was twelve years for men and thirteen years for women, notes the Census Bureau. Now it's fifteen years for men and nineteen for women. One of the prime advantages of living longer means that you have more time to learn and save for the future.

- **Your health may be good and your income higher when you are elderly.** Medicare never covered everything and probably never will. There will always be out-of-pocket health care expenses.

Better health care and more money (due to higher working incomes) to pay for it bodes well for aging baby boomers. Among noninstitutionalized persons in 1992, three in four aged 65 to 72 considered their health to be good, very good, or excellent, according to the Employee Benefit Research Institute. And those numbers will improve over time as medical technology and improved lifestyles lengthen our life spans. The over-65 generation also has seen median income more than double since 1957 to $14,548 for men and $8,189 for women. So based on that trend (if it continues), you will have more money to spend on health care. It's also likely that Congress will continue to fund Medicare and Social Security. Congress, however, will cut both programs in some way, owing to the sheer size of the baby boom generation. That's why, to blunt the costs of medical care in the future, the best strategy is to save now.

- **Coming up short? You can plan ahead now.** Are you in the one-fifth of American households that the Consumer Federation of America (CFA) says has nothing saved for major financial goals? If so, there are some immediate steps you can take. The key is financial planning, which is the primary mission of your late-start route to New Prosperity. The CFA says that those who had a financial plan had double the savings of those in the group of nonplanners. Among those households with incomes between $40,000 and $99,999, planners reported median savings of $89,650 versus $41,500 for nonplanners. Fortunately, it's never too late to plan. In fact, late starters need to plan even more carefully. I'll show you how.

- **While the cost of living rises, your expenses may drop.** If you could knock off your monthly mortgage payment (or reduce it), not worry about education bills, and trim other daily living expenses, you'd have much more money for your late-start plan. This reduction of expenses is more achievable as you get older. There's more money to save because there's less to spend it on with your home paid for and children on their own. You'll also be able to tap paid-up cash-value life insurance (if you have a policy), use home equity, and maybe see money from inheritances (this is always hard to estimate). You can also reduce your living expenses a number of ways. While health-care, transportation, and other basic costs are climbing, there's no reason you can't keep ahead just by having fewer expenses because you are older.

A Further Reality Check: Social Security's Future

Social Security, Medicare, and even private pension programs are in peril if current trends continue. That doesn't mean they can't be changed to ensure their survival, however. They can be salvaged. In order to understand how these programs might change and what impact that might have on your future, you need a brief history of the "reform movement" to put it into perspective for yourself. Once you have a clearer picture of where retirement benefits are headed, you may conclude that the best possible course is the simplest: Save as much as you can as wisely as you can.

You should not assume Social Security is a complete fallback position for your retirement or that it will disappear completely. Just expect that it won't be as generous to you as it was to your parents. As one of the largest and most successful government programs, Social Security is vulnerable to the machinations of politicians, who try to cast it as an element of the welfare state, which it isn't. Long term, it can be retooled to ensure funding for baby boomers and the generations after them. Politicians and Wall Street are loathe for you to know that, however.

LATE-STARTER TIP

If you make more, you can make the most of a late-start plan. While it may be true that late starters haven't saved much, they can still make up for lost time because of higher incomes. Reports Joyce Manchester, an analyst in the Congressional Budget Office, "looking ahead to the financial circumstances of baby boomers in retirement, it is likely that baby boomers in general will have higher real retirement incomes than older people today." Higher incomes mean greater compounding of invested assets. Moreover, making more money during peak earning years (between 35 and 55) can offset the fact that only one-third of baby boomers polled in a Merrill Lynch survey said they'd have enough "to maintain their standard of living in retirement." All told, some 18 million baby boomers are said to be at risk in the undersavings department. The advent of potentially higher-returning defined-contribution plans and many other self-directed plans is tailor made for late starters and can help close the gap.

Historically, Social Security was designed to serve as a stopgap for those who worked but didn't receive generous company pensions. It was also a social insurance program intended to act as a safety net for the elderly poor. Some sixty years ago when Social Security was created, no one envisioned how the scope of the program would expand to cover health care and disabilities and the extent to which it would buffer poverty. Even if you are starting late, you should assume that Social Security will be there for you in some form, but that you still need to save and invest as much as possible in case Social Security isn't as generous as it was for your parents. Let's take a look at the history of the system and then fast-forward to see what the future holds.

During the depths of the Great Depression, President Franklin Delano Roosevelt wanted Congress to enact a program that couldn't be touched by politicians. So in 1935 he linked his new Social Security program to payroll taxes, giving each worker a Social Security number "so that no damn politician could ever take it away."

The first benefits were paid out in lump sums averaging $58.06; the smallest payment was for 5¢. Although the program was believed to ease the unemployment of the period by giving senior citizens a small supplement for retirement, the first monthly benefits didn't begin until January 1940. Ironically, it had almost no impact on the unemployment of the time nor did it provide much for those retired. Ida May Fuller of Ludlow, Vermont, received $22.54 in the first Social Security retirement check ever cut. She died in 1975 at age 100, having collected more than $20,000 in benefits. She was a bit of an overachiever. The average life expectancy in those days was 63.

Numerous polls have shown that baby boomers and the "baby bust" generation don't believe that Roosevelt's program will be there when they retire in the next century. This mindset is transforming the economic underpinnings of American society. An explosion of do-it-yourself pension plans has emerged in the past fifteen years, largely because of tax breaks and a need to compensate for assumed future shortfalls in Social Security. Those who have taken advantage of tax-deferred plans have propelled the stock market to dizzying heights. As a result, they've been amply rewarded despite the notorious volatility of the market; however, these investors are clearly in the minority. Most Americans aged 20 to 50, surveys show, are clearly not prepared with their own pension programs, although they can reverse their course and take a different view of Social Security and their own financial future. To understand how Social Security is being downgraded as a reliable safety net, you have to understand the new war over Social Security, which is being waged using high-profile Washington think tanks and public opinion polls.

The Forces Behind Social Security "Reform"

Aside from the baby boomer retirement bulge and people just living longer, the real "third rail" that electrifies Social Security reform debates has nothing to do with either demographic issue. When an extensive analysis of documents and a cross-checking of financial records is done, it becomes clear that Social Security reform is being put on the table by large corporate financial services and other business interests in an effort to both create more wealth for businesses managing retirement funds (especially Social Security contributions in a privatized system) and deflect the public's attention from the declining tax contributions of multinational corporations. In their landmark book *America: Who Stole the Dream?* (Andrews McMeel, 1996), Pulitzer Prize winners Donald Bartlett and James Steele directly link the diminished middle-class standard of living and the attack on government "entitlement" programs such as Social Security to the increasingly smaller contribution of multinationals to the U.S. Treasury. In campaigning for balanced budgets and lower tax rates, corporations have succeeded in lowering their costs of doing business mostly through lower interest and tax rates.

Although Social Security is funded through payroll taxes by working people, corporate lobbies have reframed the impending "collapse" of the Social Security/Medicare program as a *tax* issue that imperils the economy—and their hope to further reduce *their* costs of doing business in the future. That's because shrinking federal spending, the conventional economic thinking goes, translates into lower interest rates because of lower demand for credit from the world's biggest borrower—the U.S. government. Look at how successful corporate America has been at reducing its tax burden:

> Thanks to sharply [corporate tax] lower rates and a variety of tax concessions, corporations in the 1990s pay comparatively less income tax than corporations in the 1950s. During that earlier decade, corporations accounted for 39 percent of all income tax revenue; individuals supplied 61 percent. For the years 1990 to 1995, the corporate share dropped to 19 percent, while the individual share rose to 81 percent.[1]

The cries for deficit reduction, generational equity, and a balanced budget have a hollow ring when you examine the groups producing them. To understand how the movement for the reform of Social Security evolved, you need to look at the history of the major players.

The Concord Coalition, a deficit-cutting group founded by former Senators Warren Rudman and Paul Tsongas and former Commerce Secretary Pete Peterson, is the most visible advocate for reform of Social Security. Concord, in lockstep with Third Millennium (another Peterson-funded group purportedly representing "baby busters" calling for Social Security reform), has campaigned for privatization of Social Security. Concord's original supporters read like a who's who of Wall Street and corporate influence: Archer Daniels Midland, Chemical Bank, Paine Webber, Rockwell International, First Chicago, the Blackstone Group (Pete Peterson's investment bank), Salomon Brothers, the American Council of Life Insurance, American International Group, the Rockefeller Group, and Wachovia Trust Services.[2]

So the financial services industry is a prime mover behind the proposed dismantling of Social Security. Although there has been opposition to the creation and expansion of the Social Security system since the 1930s, the most virulent opposition has taken shape during the last fifteen years or so. The most active group on this front has been the libertarian Cato Institute, a bipartisan think tank founded in 1977 that is dedicated to "more options . . . consistent with the traditional American principles of limited government, individual liberty, and peace."

Cato accepts no government funding. Its largest contributors are foundations, corporations, and individuals. Among its directors were financial industry leaders Peter Ackerman, K. Tucker Anderson, Richard Dennis, and Theodore Forstmann. But the political ties are clear. Anderson, for example, gave nearly $200,000 to house Speaker Newt Gingrich's controversial GOPAC organization, the embattled funding vehicle for a conservative privatization agenda. Other Cato sponsors include financial concerns and conservative foundations such as the Bank of America, Chase Manhattan Bank, Citicorp, Farmers Insurance, Golden Rule Insurance, Household International, the Murdock Charitable Trust, Olin Foundation, Salomon Brothers, and the Sarah Scaife Foundation.[3]

Several Cato supporters would undoubtedly benefit from the privatization of Social Security. Banks, mutual funds, investment banks, and other money managers make their money from managing large portfolios of money and charging annual fees based on the size of assets. The larger the pool of money they manage, the more money they make. These managers rarely rebate their fees if their investment expertise fails to produce positive returns for their clients. And they don't guarantee a fixed benefit indexed to inflation as Social Security in its present form does.

Cato and Concord derived a great deal of momentum from a Bipartisan Commission on Entitlement Reform, chaired by Senator Bob Kerrey and former Senator Alan Simpson. Although the commission wasn't asked to figure out how to reform Social Security, its final report was dominated by the argument for privatization, which was written and sponsored by Concord's Peterson.

The bipartisan commission's 265-page report was submitted to President Clinton in January 1995. Although the mandate of this commission was to look for ways to cut the federal budget deficit and preserve the quality of life for future generations, the report the commission produced was a diatribe against Social Security, Medicare, and other "entitlement" programs. The proposed solution was to privatize Social Security by cutting benefits and handing the money over to private investment managers. Alternatives to the privatization scheme got short shrift in this report.[4]

Joe Quinn, a professor of economics at Boston College who was on the commission staff, was among a group of staffers who had grave doubts about privatization, although "we [dissenting staffers] weren't allowed to say if it [privatization] was a good idea or a bad idea." Jill Quadagno, a professor of economics at Florida State University, noted that the commission felt like "a front for the Concord Coalition." Adds commission staffer Eric Kingson, an associate professor of social work at Boston College, the findings of the commission were "extraordinarily biased—the Concord Coalition might as well have been pulling all the levers. We [on the commission] never looked at which groups were affected [by privatization] in what ways," Kingson goes on. "There was no intention to ever do that. Entitlements are the new four-letter word."

In Washington, big issues like funding or dismantling Social Security/Medicare are never resolved quickly. Yet another commission will study the matter further beginning in 1998.

Will Private Management of Social Security Help or Hurt?

Of course there's nothing wrong with corporations and financial industry funding nonprofit public interest groups. But when those groups will directly profit from the success of the groups, there's a public-interest question at stake.

The bottom line for all of us is if the financial industry's handling of our Social Security funds (deducted from every paycheck) will make us more or less secure in the future. Before we answer that question, though, let's take a look at the money trail and see where it leads. Labor Economist Professor Theresa Guilarducci of Notre Dame University estimates that the financial industry will land a windfall of $126 billion in funds to manage (based on the 1993–96 period) if Social Security is privatized.[5] The industry's argument is that it can manage our money far better than the government, which essentially invests it in Treasury bonds. Granted, corporately managed stock mutual funds often outpace the rate of inflation, but they'll also take up to 3% (or more) of your assets per year to do it. This 3% includes management, marketing, trading, and administration expenses. If fund managers charge a front- or back-end load, or sales commission, add another 4.5%.

Now let's compare the private sector's 3% to 7% per year to what the Social Security Administration costs taxpayers to manage, administer, and distribute Social Security funds today: 0.89% per year.[6] Note where the decimal point is and the fact that every contributor's benefit is guaranteed *and* indexed to inflation. Can private industry do that? No mutual funds—and certainly no private money managers—will do it that cheaply with the guarantee and inflation indexing. Remember, if the market goes down just before you retire, you're out of luck in a private account. No one will guarantee your principal, unless of course you have invested in government bonds, which is Social Security's bread and butter. Hardly any critics of the need for reform get half the attention the critics of Social Security have received. Had I not investigated this issue for *Consumers Digest* magazine, I would still be in the "Social Security is doomed and should be privatized now" camp. The truth is that Social Security and its safety net *can* be saved without privatizing the whole system and eliminating the guarantees of this fine social insurance.

No matter what happens, though, you're better off assuming that Social Security will *not* be the linchpin of your New Prosperity, so you need to manage your money for maximum return. And you can do it paying a lot less than 3% (management fees) a year. You have plenty of time to learn, too.

Dispelling Myths about Social Security

Thanks to all the disinformation about Social Security in circulation, most Americans have accepted that the system is going broke and is on its way to extinction. The situation is not as bad as you've probably heard. Many of the statements about Social Security are patently false. Here's what the official word is (as taken from the Social Security Administration's own records):

- **Social Security is like a savings account.** No, it's neither a payroll savings plan nor a pension plan. It's a social insurance plan that was originally designed to provide supplementary income when you retired or became disabled or your spouse died during your prime working years. Pension plans, in contrast, pay based on rate of return, investment, and number of years in the plan. Social Security pays based only on your salary and age at retirement. Since Social Security taxes are primarily invested in risk-free Treasury bonds, the funds are not invested for growth, as with a pension plan. Your payroll tax may be invested or used to pay beneficiaries. It's a transfer of payments plan like any other insurance plan. To understand this idea, think of what happens if your house burns down: your premiums and those of others who have policies with your homeowners' insurance company will go to pay your claim.

- **I should get paid everything I paid into it.** This is true for some workers, but certainly not for all. Keep in mind that the system has been expanded dramatically from its inception in 1935. The first recipient was Ernest Ackerman, who got a check for 17¢ when he retired in 1940. Of course those who are retiring soon will live to receive more than they put in. Younger or highly paid workers may never get back their total contributions. Why the disparity? Because, as an insurance program, Social Security pools money for those who need it. It's similar to health insurance. When you get sick, you are subsidized by healthy people, who don't use the benefits and pay into a pool through their premiums. With Social Security, *you* pay into the system when you're working. When you retire or become disabled, you receive a fixed benefit. So you're insured, but are not able to access all of the money through a lump-sum payout as you could from a private retirement plan. If the system was changed to allow you to withdraw all the funds you put into the system at once, everybody would pull their money out and the system would go broke overnight.

- **Social Security benefits only the rich elderly.** Wrong. As a social insurance program, Social Security covers every worker along with their dependents. But Social Security benefits far more than the elderly. The average age of *disabled* workers covered by the system was 49.7 years (in 1994), according to the agency. In fact, 66% of disabled workers were under age 62. Moreover, as of December 1994, some 3 million children received benefits, about half of them because their parents died. Additionally, 3.2 million blind and disabled adults under 65 receive benefits, as well as 3.9 million disabled workers, 618,000 disabled children, and 161,000 disabled widows and widowers.

- **The Social Security trust funds are being raided by the government.** The money's there, but understanding how it's used is the subject of much debate. Your payroll taxes—which amount to some $5 billion per month for all employed Americans—go into a reserve account. These funds are then invested in special-issue U.S. Treasury bonds, which constitute the Social Security "Trust Fund." Although these bonds are unmarketable—you can't take them to a bank to cash them in—they are protected from market and credit risk. Some critics of these bonds claim that these are just government IOUs. Technically, the critics are correct. The government converts your payroll dollars into bonds, which are promises to repay a debt at a future date. But to date, the government has never defaulted on a Treasury bond. If it did, the *world* financial network would probably collapse, and you'd have a few more problems to worry about than Social Security. The Social Security trust fund has built up a reserve of several billion dollars, which will more than cover benefits for the next thirty years. But due to a demographic reality that will see more retirees than workers, the trust fund will run a deficit unless new funding solutions are found. The government does in fact use the cash from payroll taxes to run its business, but the T-bonds replacing that cash are perhaps the most secure, interest-bearing investments in the world. A dirty little secret of government accounting is that the Social Security surplus covers much of the federal deficit.

- **I could do better than Social Security if I could invest my payroll taxes.** Well, perhaps you could, but most people don't. And you sure wouldn't be able to get through the private sector what Social Security offers now. Keep in mind that your payroll taxes provide the equivalent of a $295,000 life insurance policy if you have a spouse and two children; a $203,000 disability policy with the same family; and a retirement income plan that pays up to $1,248 per month (a maximum benefit for someone retiring in January 1996 at age 65). All of these benefits are essentially guaranteed—unless Congress restructures the program. The notion that Social Security is an investment of your money is also patently false. It's simply a protected pooling to help you out if you become disabled and you need extra income when you retire. Congress is mandated by law to preserve the solvency of the program; however, in recent years it has cut benefits to cover shortfalls in funding. Since its inception, the program has expanded to include expensive benefits such as Medicare and disability. So the payroll taxes you and others contribute constitute

SOCIAL SECURITY IS STILL A BIG PIECE OF THE RETIREMENT PIE

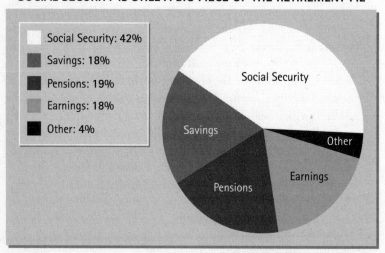

Social Security: 42%
Savings: 18%
Pensions: 19%
Earnings: 18%
Other: 4%

SOURCE: Susan Grad, *Income of the Population 55 or Older, 1994* (Washington, D.C.: SSA, Office of Research and Statistics, 1996).

an insurance fund that must cover increasingly costlier medical expenses for a growing number of people. For the money, there simply is no private counterpart to what Social Security provides. There's also nothing stopping you from investing in your own pension plan, 401(k), IRA, Keogh, SEP-IRA, Roth IRA, or annuity to add to your future Social Security income.

- **Social Security adds to the federal deficit.** Clearly not true now, although in 2030, that may be the case. Since the system is running a more than $70 billion surplus—and will do so through 2013—the Social Security system is *adding* money to the government's balance sheet. In fact, if the surplus from the Social Security system was removed from the government's accounting of the federal deficit, the shortfall would be much higher.

What the Social Security Fallout Means to You

Believing that they will not have a retirement safety net, two generations are intensively looking to private-market solutions for their nest eggs. Their pessimism is fueling one of the greatest bull stock markets in history. Thousands of mutual funds, annuities, life insurance products and tax-deferred vehicles are being redesigned for more than 90 million Americans with one thing on their minds: Social Security will be defunct, so no more retirement safety net. Whether that is actually the case, an outright lie, or a self-fulfilling prophecy has really become moot.

The combination of a reform-minded Congress and Americans' doubts about the system will ultimately force Social Security to be less generous and private options such as 401(k)s and IRAs to be more flexible. The 1997 tax reforms alone provided several new vehicles and opportunities to save money while deferring taxes. In the larger picture, the private sector wins big—and you can, too.

More important, Americans are moving away from the New Deal into a "My Deal" mindset: self-reliance in investing and financial services. This will set the stage for one of the greatest transformations of world financial markets in modern history. There's no reason you can't be a part of this worldwide boom.

Getting Beyond Social Security: Why You Need to Take Action Now

The advice for a "conventional" retirement used to be succinct. Save as much as you could and supplement it with Social Security and your company pension. These three legs of the retirement stool have been partially cut off, however. Nearly half of American workers don't even have a company pension and big companies are moving to cut benefits for their retired employees. So how do you plan to be comfortably situated in a time of corporate downsizing, an embattled Social Security program, and a tough environment in which to save?

To a large extent, you'll need to take inventory of your life. There is a New Prosperity out there that goes beyond pensions, vacation homes, and boats and cars. It may involve some restructuring on your part, but it could amount to a new life beyond corporate America that will satisfy your longings for comfort, security, and community.

You can join the New Prosperity movement as you age. The motto of this movement is self-reliance, responsibility, and spirituality. Noble sentiments, you're thinking, but how does this square with an economic reality that is increasingly hostile to a smooth path to a secure retirement? Why do you need to act now? Let's look at the facts:

- Case in point: U.S. workers are working one month longer each year than in 1967 (and taking fewer vacations) but we're earning less in today's dollars. In fact, to afford that dream home in the suburbs, we're putting in more time commuting (nine hours a week) than in overtime (five hours), according to *Labor Notes*. So it's not surprising that because they are working more and getting less, tens of millions are saying, "Okay, I've had enough, how do I get out of this trap?" Ironically, though, most of us are working more to keep up with the bills. Although inflation has hovered below 4.5 percent in the 1990s, local taxes, college tuition, and the price of big-ticket items such as cars and homes have nearly doubled. At the beginning of the decade, you could buy a basic car (a compact) for about $10,000. Now the price tag is closer to

$20,000. Granted, today's car is arguably safer and more efficient than its 1990 counterpart, but is this basic transportation worth twice as much? Although the price of everything is going up, you can manage to live the kind of life you want to live if you manage your expenditures a little better. Subsequent chapters will show you how.

- Large numbers of people are spending less—living the frugal life. The Trends Institute has found that some 15% of the 77 million baby boomers are now actively participating in this trend. The reason is simple: More people want more out of life with fewer material trappings. Reduced corporate benefits and a higher cost of living (taxes, housing, etc.) are forcing Americans to do more with less. Simplicity is more than just spending less on things you may not need. It's taking a holistic view of your life and how you value it. I'll show you how to do that.

- Massive shifts in society are prompting a focus on value—value shifting—in which people will buy fewer things but will demand higher quality. That means traditional retirement is out the door. It's no longer a divine American right that you will work for one company for thirty or forty years and then retire to tend to the grandkids, the golf course, or the beach. Value shifting has more to do with how you live than what you buy. You may have to abandon that "shop 'til you drop" consumerist ethic if you want to live comfortably and achieve the new prosperity. You'll need to ask some hard questions and seek new approaches to your spending and lifestyle in general.

Although you may be starting late, the basic work you need to do will not take long. If you're going to invest for the long term, think and plan for the long term.

Myths About Pension Security: Why Your Company Pension Isn't What You Think

Now that you understand the direction society and Social Security are taking, you need to take a more realistic view of what your company will do for you. Like Social Security, conventional private company pensions are not going to be what they were for your parents. Imagine you worked for a company and had a generous pension plan and other fringe benefits secured by a union contract; your union lawyer was one of the most powerful politicians in your city. Then one day, due to bad luck, a recession, and shortsighted management, your company files for bankruptcy. You have nothing to worry about because your benefits are backed up not only by that union contract and that powerful union lawyer, but by the government as well.

Frank Lumpkin and thousands of his coworkers were employed at Wisconsin Steel Works in March 1980 and had plenty of reasons to be confident. After all, politicians in Southeast Chicago were thrown out of town if they let their constituents go hungry. While the mills breathed smoke, the Chicago political machine and local businesses hummed with activity. So when padlocks were slapped on the mill's gates (the mill was never to reopen), the workers believed government would come to their aid. They were the heart and soul of the largest steel-producing region of the time. The steel they made went into tractors built by International Harvester, one of the largest and oldest industrial combines. Their labor, taxes, and votes kept the city running smoothly.

Unfortunately, when the mill's gates were closed for good, hundreds of men who had less than twenty years in the mill got nothing—no pensions, back pay, vacation pay, or any of the other benefits guaranteed by their union contract. When the government's pension insurance agency, the Pension Benefit Guaranty Corporation (PBGC), finally stepped in, it provided only small amounts for those vested (meeting complex service and age requirements) in the plan. Lumpkin and a group of fellow workers were forced to sue the company, International Harvester, and other parties to collect what they were owed. Some seventeen years later, they won a few dollars in a settlement from Harvester, now renamed Navistar, which was paid in the form of Navistar stock, selling for under $10 a share. Some 350 workers would never see any money, having died in virtual poverty. Of the $60 million owed the workers by the company, only $17 million was paid after more than a decade and a half of worker-initiated lawsuits.

Frank Lumpkin's tale is not an isolated anecdote of an industrial America that seems to have gone the way of disco, leveraged buy-outs, and pet rocks. Some 60% of Americans have no private pension, according to the U.S. Department of Labor. With a work-force increasingly white collar, temporary, or displaced, that figure is probably understated. The largest employer in America (as of this writing) is not U.S. Steel, Exxon, or General Motors. It's Man-power, Inc., a temporary help agency. Given these trends, it's clear that new pension plans are not likely to offer fixed benefits. Most are defined contribution, meaning the amount you receive at re-tirement is entirely dependent upon how you manage your money in a number of mutual funds your company offers.

So the bad news is that companies are providing less and less in terms of secure, guaranteed benefits. The good news is that if you don't have a pension, you can set up your own. There have never been more options with which to save and invest for the future than there are today. Late-start investors are particularly blessed, because they will not have to wait as long as those in previous gen-erations to enjoy tax-free or penalty-free withdrawals from their pension plans. These plans have relatively simple rules and can be set up in an hour or less. The investments contained within them are generally accessible by making a few phone calls.

What This Book Will Teach You

Lifestyle Planning

This book will show you how to define what a New Prosperity can mean for you and how to obtain it. Part of retirement planning in-volves getting savvy about what you're spending. It's surprising how much money you can free up for investing if you revise your cur-rent spending habits.

Investing with Purpose

There are only a few ways of doing this right, so this book will sug-gest a few mutual funds, stocks, and other vehicles to put some cash in the kitty. Company retirement plans are a big player in gaining your new prosperity.

Investing in Yourself

Sure, you can bulk up on the best-performing stocks and mutual funds, but you've also got to invest in yourself. This book will show you how to get your mind and heart to where they need to be in order to achieve a new prosperity. It's all part of the plan.

If time is short, can you do it? Will you have to take unnecessary risks to achieve a comfortable retirement? After all, the stock market tanks from time to time. Inflation may rear its ugly head. Interest rates tick up and bonds will lose money. There's going to be another conflict in the Middle East and the market won't like it. Aren't you better off just sticking money under your mattress or investing in insured certificates of deposit? Not necessarily. This book provides a simple strategy to avoid some of the volatility in the market. There *is* a better way, and it's so painless and profitable that Wall Street would tremble if most investors followed it.

This book will also help you make basic lifestyle changes so that you can prepare yourself for any number of retirement options. This book will help you "right-size" your expenses and still meet your goals. Both stocks and mutual funds will be profiled, using the latest in financial research that combines low-risk management with high returns, defying market cycles and earnings surprises.

Lifestyle Management and Retirement

Those who want to invest want to improve or maintain a lifestyle. Those who just want a lifestyle rarely invest. The latter group works like dogs to pay off bills and don't get to enjoy what they have—or think they need. This is a book for people who want to invest in something but haven't quite identified what yet. In many cases, investment may not take the form of monetary growth. It may be investing in yourselves.

We've reached the end of an age. The pressures of life, living for the almighty dollar, and paying off ever-accumulating debts have gotten to us. We've become like machines in a machine age, needing constant maintenance so that we can consume the energy created by our labors. There's a reason why there's expansive growth in entertainment, travel, and gambling. We want to be distracted from our machine-like existence, which is neither fulfilling nor rewarding. It's accepted that most American parents will probably spend more time shuttling around in their minivans or sports utility vehicles than talking to their children or doing something for themselves. What kind of life is that?

We want to escape, but how? Personal bankruptcies topped the 1 million mark in 1997 for the first time in history.[7] Consumer debt has never been higher. Despite a lack of real inflation, wages are stagnant and corporate America is downsizing. For many, the way out is Prozac, credit cards, and mass denial. If those quick remedies worked, at least we'd feel better. Take a look around and you'll quickly conclude that the answer to our troubles is elusive.

Retirement used to be the great antidepressant of life's journey. No more bosses, no more time clocks, no more annual reviews. No more work. How, we may ask, can we afford to retire if there are still taxes to pay, car payments to make, and food to put on the table today? What's left over for the golden years? Can there be such a thing as old-age prosperity when pensions, Social Security, and a lack of savings are leaving us in the lurch? Yes. Although you may need to make some difficult decisions, you *can* achieve a new prosperity.

Your New Prosperity

There's much more to retirement than investing in stocks, bonds, or real estate. There are dreams, ideas, and ourselves. You're in for a rekindling of the self-reliance and creativity that lies within you. What I have to share is a plan of action that works. You'll meet people who hit some obstacles in their quest for the new prosperity—people you won't find on the cover of financial magazines, but whose lives and stories offer parables about what we need in order to form a healthy relationship with our goals and money.

Summary: If You Do Nothing Else

1. Assume that Social Security *will not* form the lion's share of your retirement income. Plan accordingly.

2. Assume that your company pensions will not be as generous as those your parents received. Save and invest on your own as much as you can.

3. Get your own house in order. What do you want in terms of a New Prosperity? A warmer climate? Part-time work? A flexible job?

CHAPTER 2

Your New Prosperity Goals

How Much Do You Need? How Much Do You Have? How Do You Reach Your Goals?

"Bad carpenters blame their tools; honest carpenters blame their measurements."

If we were running our lives as a big corporation or a government agency runs itself, life would be much simpler. We could budget a few years into the future based on projected revenues and expenses. Your spreadsheet would lay out your information neatly for you. You could account for everything from paper supplies to the taxes you paid on your employees. If a recession or something else unexpected happened, you'd just rejigger your numbers and lay off a few employees to balance the books or blame the president or political party in power at the time. Unfortunately, when it comes to real life, nothing works out so neatly. Planning is difficult and fortunes change without warning.

Just ask Tom Landoch. At 52, he's just beginning to fund his retirement. The path behind him has been anything but conven-

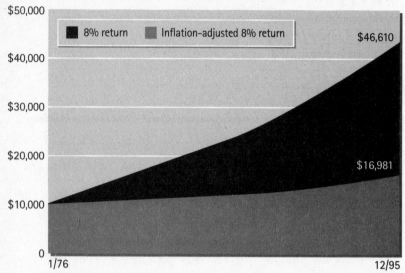

WHY YOU NEED TO INVEST:
INFLATION EATS AWAY AT LONG-TERM SAVINGS

The Inflation Factor: 8% Return on $10,000 Investment (Jan. 1976–Dec. 1995)

■ 8% return   ■ Inflation-adjusted 8% return

$50,000
$46,610
$40,000
$30,000
$20,000
$16,981
$10,000
0
1/76   12/95

SOURCE: U.S. Department of Labor Statistics. This chart uses a hypothetical investment solely to illustrate the potential effects of inflation based on stated assumptions.

tional. The son of a window washer, he's secured for himself the home he wanted in a Chicago suburb, put four children through Catholic school and college, and is just settling down with Karen, his wife of thirty-two years, to enjoy golf and the occasional excursion to a casino boat. Despite his travails, he looks ten years younger than his age.

There was a time when Tom was savoring the rewards of his intelligence, management acumen, and personality. At the end of the 1970s, when he was in his late thirties, Tom was making $55,000 a year and had two company cars and an upper-level management position with a family-owned metal-grinding company on the Northwest Side of Chicago. When the recession of 1979–81 hit, the finances of the company became shaky after the original owner died. Being the loyal employee he was, though, Tom lent $20,000 to the company with the understanding that he would be paid back in an equity stake, making him a part owner. As comptroller and vice president, he thought the risk was justified. He had four children in Catholic school and a tuition bill of $10,000 a year, which he weighed in making the decision.

Tom's goodwill and loan did not help the company, however, which was later sold to a competitor. The new bosses didn't appreciate Tom's loyalty and didn't offer him an ownership stake. They did offer him a job, however, at $35,000 a year with no company cars. After thirty-five years in a business, Tom was starting over. He originally refused to work with the new company during the transition and looked elsewhere. But every lead he had turned sour. There weren't too many openings in 1980 for men of his experience and salary demands in an economy that was devastating to old-line industrial firms large and small. It was a time when foreign competition, a discounted dollar on world exchanges, and tight money and credit forced hundreds of thousands of workers out of jobs. Nearly every worker in the so-called smokestack industries felt the pain.

In the midst of this unexpected turn in the nation's economy, Tom Landoch was at a perilous intersection in life. No avenue looked promising. After three months, Tom decided to eat his pride and take the job he was originally offered with the acquiring company. Unfortunately, by then the company had given the job to another man.

At this point, Tom was forced to liquidate almost everything he had short of his home. He cashed in all of his insurance, certificates of deposit, and other savings just to live. "I was overqualified and nobody wanted to pay me [what I thought I was worth]," he recalls. His retirement savings were gone when he took a job selling steel for $28,000 a year, a position that came with no pension. Karen found a job as a cosmetologist to help ends meet. Tom and Karen's children still had to get through college. Since they were all born within five years of one another, at some point they would all be in school *at the same time.* "It was about this time that I joked that the only way the kids were going to college would be if I shot myself. Karen wanted to go back to the city and get a less expensive house. I couldn't work another job. I was already working ten to twelve hours a day. It was too demanding."

To save money, Tom suggested state colleges for the children. Karen thought that the Catholic colleges, although they were more expensive, would be a better option. Although they didn't have the money to pay for tuition, the fact that all of the children were straight-A students and loved school—an attitude Tom attributes to Karen's influence—meant that they all qualified for scholarships. The children all chose to go to the same school, Marquette University, a Jesuit college in Milwaukee. When everyone was in school at the same time, tuition cost $50,000 a year. The children were all willing to work for their education and supplemented their financial needs with loans. Tom even wrote to the president of Marquette, stressing his unique circumstances, which included four children in the same college at once. The college knocked off $500 a year per child to ease the burden. Of course, there were semesters when Tom just didn't have the money for tuition, for which there was some forbearance on the part of the university as well. It didn't help that once the kids outgrew the dorms, they insisted on their own apartments in Milwaukee, meaning he was paying three rents in addition to his own mortgage. When Tom and Karen bought their home for $57,000 in the 1970s, little did they know that he would be borrowing against it to pay for a $1,500-a-month tuition bill when the mortgage payment was only $220 a month. Although he owed only $10,000 on the house when the college bills starting rolling in, Tom soon found himself back in the hole again with a second mortgage. And when his daughter Jackie, the oldest, left college, the first thing she wanted to do was get married, which meant Tom spent another $5,000 he didn't have.

"I always wanted to have money in my pocket. I started washing dishes when I was twelve. It scared me when I couldn't pay the bills," he said, reminiscing about that tough period in his life.

About twelve years ago, when finances could not have been tighter, the mid-level position that had gone to another man opened up, so Tom went back to the metal-grinding company. As an inside sales manager, he would have to work long hours and the pay would be much less than what he was used to as an executive. The new position, however, offered something more: a 401(k) profit-sharing plan. That meant he could start saving again for retirement and the company would kick in some of its profits to match his contribution (8% of the first 25% of his contribution).

After spending some $225,000 on tuition, Tom is satisfied with the results. Jackie, 30, is a teacher with three children. Tim, 29, is a certified public accountant, as is Troy, 27. Todd, 28, is a veterinarian. Having only begun to consider the prospect of retirement six years ago, Tom is now maxing out his 401(k) by putting away 10% of his annual salary in growth-stock mutual funds. He's also invested on the side in high-dividend stocks like Philip Morris and growth and income mutual funds. Educating himself further through financial seminars and classes, Tom is now able to work the numbers in his favor, estimating that his retirement funds will hit about $500,000 when he retires at the current rate of return (about 12% a year). He figures he and Karen can live comfortably on $60,000 a year and he can use home equity to borrow against if money ever gets tight.

Despite being on track again, Tom doesn't feel he needs $1 million in the bank, nor is he obsessed with his new financial plan. He looks at his 82-year-old father, living in a government-subsidized apartment building on Social Security and a small pension. "I don't want that. Now that I have a little money, I want to spend it. I don't want to die with $1 million in the bank," Tom says, referring to his desire to enjoy his prosperity during his lifetime.

"I've seen people with hundreds of thousands of dollars sitting in nursing homes, where the nursing homes took their life savings. I'd rather be smoking cigars, golfing, and boating at 105. I'll probably live to be 100."

Tom is proud of having raised happy and productive children. But he doesn't expect his children to take care of him when he retires and is looking forward to buying a summer home near a golf course or a condo in Florida.

"Of course I want more money and want our life to be easier, but I'm not driven by money. My wife and I aren't driven by material things. We know where our money comes from and where it goes. We also know that the more we save, the more it'll multiply."

If, like Tom Landoch, you've faced Job-like obstacles to getting on a firm financial footing, there's some solace. As we've noted, longer lives, better health care, and numerous options in self-directed pension plans can get you the time and funding for your new prosperity plan. You can start planning today and achieve results, but first you have to disavow yourself of the "traditional" model of retirement.

The Basic Myths of Retirement Planning

There must be hundreds of brochures, textbooks, and Internet sites that show you the conventional but ultimately useless way of figuring out your retirement needs. All of them use the archaic model that assumes you'll retire at 65 with X amount of pension, Social Security, and savings. Unfortunately, as Tom Landoch and millions of other real people have found out, life isn't quite that simple. There are so many detours that a "one size fits all" formula just doesn't work for most people.

Social Security and Medicare will undoubtedly be changed in some way by Congress. You may be faced with the prospect of paying to care for your parents, your siblings, and possibly your own children. Then there's the question of how to pay for health care and how long you expect to live. Most models for retirement planning assume you will be in perfect health until you die, all of your health-care expenses and those of your loved ones will be covered, and you can safely predict how much money you'll need based on variables you can't control. Here are some of the thornier issues of retirement:

- Only 30% of those surveyed by the Employee Benefit Research Institute (EBRI) said they were very confident that they would have enough money to live comfortably in retirement. Those who lacked confidence said their major concerns were medical expenses, Social Security/Medicare, and a lack of financial planning on their part.[1]

- Of those currently retired, the EBRI study said that "almost half of them were forced to retire before they planned. For these people, there was no chance for them to complete their financial plan." Corporate downsizings, health problems, and forced early retirements are believed to be behind this development.[2]

- People are retiring earlier (median age 63 in 1990 versus 67 in 1950), but are also returning to the workforce. A Pennsylvania State University study of men over a seventeen-year period found that one-third of them returned to work at some point, most coming back in the first year of retirement. This trend was most pronounced among professionals, salespeople, farm laborers, and the self-employed. Although the traditional idea of retirement is appealing, it's not for everyone. Many find fulfillment and self-worth in their work.[3]

- Disability may force you out of the workforce. The Social Security Administration (SSA) found that 35% of men who left their last job before age 55 said health was the primary reason. Although companies may cover early retirement with disability plans in tandem with Social Security, there's still a shortfall if you must leave the workforce for health reasons.[4]

- Women are in a different situation if they are dependent upon their husbands' pensions or have had sporadic work histories. That means lower benefits from the government and private sector. Although more women are working and receiving full benefits than ever before, some 39% of women aged 62 or older were receiving benefits based on their husbands' employment, according to the SSA. That compares to 57% dependent on spousal benefits in 1960.[5]

- Middle-aged Americans in their peak earning years have other things to worry about. Some six out of ten baby boomer households still have children, according to the Census Bureau. And the priority in these households is not retirement, it's paying for a college education, which can cost anywhere from $40,000 to $80,000 for a bachelor's degree in today's dollars, and maintaining their current standard of living.[6]

- Few people enjoyed retirement a generation ago because life spans were a lot shorter. Although most people surveyed think their post-work years will range between 11 and 20 years, the average number of years of life remaining after 65 is *17.2* years, according to EBRI. Nobody plans to be old these days, but life spans are growing longer and you'll need a bigger nest egg.[7]

EXPECTED YEARS IN RETIREMENT

Retirement Age	Individual	Couple (same age)
55	29 years	34 years
60	24 years	30 years
65	20 years	25 years
70	16 years	21 years

SOURCE: IRS Life Expectancy Tables. If you have a spouse/companion, odds are you'll live even longer in retirement.

So how do you plan when you can't predict your future health, don't know if the government safety net will be fully intact, and have no idea how much money you'll need when you get there? The best way to solve this problem is to view it as a trip, mapping out your destinations. As is true of any great trip, there are plenty of diversions that may deter you from your ultimate goal. The remarkable thing about this journey is that you learn every step of the way.

New Prosperity Destinations: An Itinerary

What's the first thing to do before you take a trip? You check your transportation resources. If you're driving, you gas up, check the oil, and make sure engine parts aren't flying off. If you're taking a limo to the airport, you call and confirm. If you're taking a train or bus, you check to see that you're leaving the house with the tickets. The road to New Prosperity requires such a check. Only this road check requires a little more homework. The following are the most basic resources you need to consider:

- **How much will you receive from Social Security?** How much are you owed if you retire early or retire at 67 or later? See page 49 for how to check this information for free. Despite what you hear about Social Security, income from this system constitutes primary retirement income for 63% of Americans, according to EBRI and the National Academy on Aging. The more you've made over the years and the longer you've worked, the higher the monthly benefit. Social Security will be around in some form, so don't count it out. The full retirement age to receive maximum monthly benefits is changing, depending on your date of birth.

WHEN YOU CAN COLLECT FULL SOCIAL SECURITY BENEFITS

If your birth date is . . .	Then "full" retirement age is . . .
1/2/38–1/1/39	65 years and 2 months
1/2/39–1/1/40	65 years and 4 months
1/2/40–1/1/41	65 years and 6 months
1/2/41–1/1/42	65 years and 8 months
1/2/42–1/1/43	65 years and 10 months
1/2/43–1/1/55	66 years
1/2/55–1/1/56	66 years and 2 months
1/2/56–1/1/57	66 years and 4 months
1/2/57–1/1/58	66 years and 6 months
1/2/58–1/1/59	66 years and 8 months
1/2/59–1/1/60	66 years and 10 months
1/2/60 and later	67 years

SOURCE: *Social Security Handbook,* Section 723

- **How much money do you have now?** This is like checking your wallet before you leave on a trip. Your own assets are like your traveler's checks. Anything you have in savings accounts, bonds, stocks, home equity, personal collectibles, and inheritances due is part of your traveling money. If you want to subtract what you owe (mortgage balance, loans, etc.) from what you own, you have either a positive or a negative *net worth*. This is a term used by financial planners to scare us into believing we are worthless. Don't take this number seriously. Life changes. Kids leave college and home. You can pay off your mortgage. You can cut your living expenses in hundreds of ways in order to boost your savings. Like all of the figures in this chapter, this one should be regarded like a billboard on the side of the road. Once you pass it up, you forget all about it. It's the total of your assets that are important. Some 25% of Americans' retirement funds are from their own savings, according to the Social Security Administration.

- **How much do you have coming from your company retirement plan?** If you have a defined-benefit plan and plan to retire after thirty years, this is a no-brainer. Your personnel department will give you an exact dollar amount. Defined-contribution plans like 401(k)s and 403(b)s in which you control how money is invested in mutual funds are a bit trickier. Your totals here depend on what you invest in (stocks, bonds, money-market funds), how well those investments do over time, and if you keep the money in the plan. Some 18% of retirement funds come from company pension plans and 12% from wage earnings. If you make more money or contribute more, you can reason that your New Prosperity fund will be larger.

- **What other sources of money do you have?** This is money you create through lifestyle decisions or through savings. You can sell your house and buy a condo in a low-cost, Sunbelt retirement mecca. You can sell one car for cash or buy used ones. You can convince your kids to attend community colleges and save 50% on the first two years of college. This list is endless, but you get the idea. Any personal discretionary money gets you to your destination quicker.

Diversions and How to Deal with Setbacks

The primary reason that you can't plan exactly how much you'll need in retirement is that life doesn't follow any budget or plan. There are many detours. Jobs are lost. Parents may need nursing-home care. You may have a disabled child or suffer a work-ending disability yourself. Some things you *can* see coming, so plan accordingly. If you know a loved one will need to be institutionalized, find out what government programs can help. The best sources of information for this dilemma are your congressional representative, your local library, and the Internet. Here are a few more basics to consider before you even start running the numbers on the remainder of your New Prosperity plan:

- **You and your spouse/significant other should get a thorough physical exam that will check for maladies present in your family.** Say your family is subject to a debilitating lung disease. Check for it now. Unreimbursed medical expenses in the future can derail your plan. Extensive tests can be taken for hundreds of chronic diseases and conditions. I've had several friends who've gone to their doctors regularly, checking for potentially fatal conditions such as melanomas and prostate conditions. Consistent medical care that includes regular checkups, tests, and a wellness program (a low-fat, high-fiber diet combined with regular exercise) can help stem costly or fatal lifestyle-related diseases.

- **Are your parents in good health?** How would you take care of them if they were subject to a long-term debilitating illness? Do they have resources of their own? What would you do if they had to go to a nursing home? Do they have decent long-term care insurance that covers home care and will keep pace with inflation? Will they have enough assets if they don't have insurance? Despite what you may think, there is no middle-class government program that will pay for quality custodial care. Medicare covers only hospitals and medical services (after a 20% out-of-pocket deductible). Their lack of resources could eat into *your* retirement savings. If you haven't talked to your parents about this subject, now's the time.

- **Are your children provided for?** This means having a will or living trust and life insurance if your children are still at home and dependent upon your income. Special arrangements (such as supplementary needs trusts) need to be made for disabled children. See an experienced estate-planning lawyer if you wish to devise such a trust. Now is not the time to worry about how much you're going to leave your children. If you're reading this book, you have to take care of No. 1 first. Don't feel selfish about it, either. Do you want your children or other relatives to have to take care of you?

- **How's your job outlook?** This has been such a wild card over the past twenty years that it's akin to one's health. Certain factors are predictable, others are not. If you're in a dying profession, an industry undergoing wrenching change, or a company in the midst of restructuring, ask yourself "What would I do to make money if I lost my job?" For some, that means starting a business on the side, going back to school to learn new skills, or simply cutting back on lifestyle expenses (eating out, lavish vacations, etc.). If you're not working, you're not saving.

The Ultimate Destination: How Much Will You Need?

This is the part where you add up some numbers and, based on how you are living and want to live in the future, decide if you're making enough money to achieve that goal of New Prosperity. The key to making this decision is to see how much you have and how much you expect to have and decide how you want to live. Read chapters 3 and 10 before you reach any conclusions. If you're getting antsy, however, the following table will give you some guidelines about where you stand. Again, these numbers are based on *averages,* and I've yet to find an average family.

The table on page 43 is a thumbnail sketch of how much extra money you'll need if you want to live pretty much the same way you're living now. Of course, in the future, most of your bills will be lower, so this is just an estimate. First, match your annual gross (before taxes) income with your age and read to the right.

This table is based on the assumption you'll be in retirement for at least fifteen years starting at age 65 and want to cut back maybe 30% in terms of income in retirement. Your retirement kitty will be supplemented by maximum Social Security benefits and a modest pension. So this table shows how much you'll need to save on your own above and beyond Social Security and a private pension—if you want to maintain a lifestyle similar to your current standard of living. Don't be put off by these numbers. You still have time to plan. This is just a general guideline, *not* the final pronouncement on how much you should be saving. You'll need to read the next two chapters to decide if you are going to make lifestyle changes and where you can save money. There is much you can do if you think you're going to come up short.

WHAT WILL IT TAKE TO MAINTAIN YOUR CURRENT STANDARD OF LIVING IN RETIREMENT (GIVEN CURRENT INCOME)?

Current Age	Current Income	Additional Funds Needed
40	$120,000	$2,280,161
	$80,000	$1,407,087
	$40,000	$552,839
50	$120,000	$1,312,274
	$80,000	$776,278
	$40,000	$251,842
60	$120,000	$737,095
	$80,000	$408,049
	$40,000	$85,024

NOTES: The American Savings Education Council, which prepared this table, makes a few assumptions. First, they assume you'll be in retirement for fifteen years, there's a 4% annual inflation rate and a modest 4% annual growth rate in income. So this is a baseline estimate that your income is just keeping even with inflation at roughly today's rates. Then this model assumes you'll be living at 70% of your present level of income with maximum Social Security benefits and pension equal to 35% of your retirement income. By the way, this model also assumes you're also in a 28% tax bracket and are making an 8% pretax return on your investments.

Don't base your New Prosperity plan exclusively on these numbers. These are just benchmarks to tell you if you are close or way off. If you are not even close, there are dozens of simple adjustments you can make to cut your spending or boost savings. You'll need to know if your standard of living/need for income will decline significantly or will change due to "wild-card" expenses. It also helps to define what New Prosperity will mean for you. For more on that, jump to the next chapter.

Quick Fixes for Late Starters

Here are some ways of "cooking the books" in your favor. They are expounded upon in Chapter 5 on page 105 and could make your trip to a New Prosperity a lot smoother:

- **Trim your biggest expenses first.** You can pay off your mortgage, reduce property taxes, or sell your home and move somewhere less expensive. Housing expenses are probably your largest monthly bill now. If you're getting a late start on funding your New Prosperity plan, trimming these bills can put a lot of money in your pocket to invest. If you can live in a smaller home, recent changes in the tax laws will give most of you a break on capital gains when you sell your house.

- **Consider rental real estate.** Move out of your home, but don't sell it. Rent it out for positive cash flow and move into smaller quarters where the property taxes are lower. Also consider investing in other rental real estate if you can manage to turn a profit and want to be a landlord.

- **Cash in your life insurance policy.** If you have a paid-up cash-value life insurance policy and no dependents, cash it in or borrow against it for money to invest. See your insurance agent for details. There's no reason to have life insurance if you have no dependents. Life insurance is not an investment. It costs too much and pays you too little; only your agent and insurer will make money from it if you have no dependents.

- **Figure out your investment returns now.** Calculate best-, medium-, and worst-case scenarios for returns on your money. A whole host of free Internet calculators (see http://www.financenter.com) can help you figure (1) the ravages of inflation over time, (2) the value of compounding, and (2) future values based on average rates of return. If you want to take the risk (and you will need to take some risk to increase the size of your nest egg in a short period of time), consider the best-performing stocks and mutual funds (see chapters 7 and 8).

- **Downsize your transportation budget.** Get rid of one car or buy used cars. At this stage of the game, why pay $400 to $1,000 a month just for something you can't live in, you won't keep, and that's constantly in need of repair while it depreciates in value. If you can downsize your transportation budget, you can immediately put the savings into your New Prosperity plan.

- **Downsize your amenities budget.** Simply look at what you're spending each month on things you can live without: expensive meals, cable television, clothing, vacations. Collect receipts, audit your credit-card bills, and scan your checking-account expenditures. There are instant savings here. This is where most late starters can turn up big savings fast.

- **Stop shopping for shopping's sake.** Go into every store with lists for things you need and don't buy anything not on them. Impulse buying can drag down your New Prosperity plan. Save more, buy less. No store will ever use this as its slogan, but you can.

Fill in the Blanks:
Doing the Numbers for Your New Prosperity

Let's see how much you have. This is the simplest math you'll ever do and perhaps the clearest indication of where you stand financially. You'll need to total up your *liquid* assets, meaning anything that's worth money that can be sold today. Not all of these assets figure into a formula for your New Prosperity, so we'll have to look at those items in a different light.

Your home and autos can't be easily cashed in tomorrow, so they tend to be *illiquid*. These assets can't be sold easily and you don't know exactly what you'll get for them. It may take weeks or months to get what you want for them and some markets may not net you the selling price you think is fair. So let's start with the basics:

New Prosperity Worksheets

What You Own Now: Somewhat Illiquid Assets

Home Equity This includes your down payment, improvements made, principal owned plus market value.   _____

Auto Equity If your car is currently financed, subtract the principal and the down payment from what you owe the banks.   _____

"Found" Money: Other Illiquid Intangibles This includes a legal settlement due, an expected inheritance, a workman's compensation claim, or expected alimony. These are items that aren't sure things, but those you suspect will be coming soon.   _____

Other Real-Estate Equity List rental real estate, condos, vacation homes, or time-shares.   _____

SUBTOTAL ILLIQUID ASSETS   _____

Liquid Assets: Things You Can Easily Sell Tomorrow Individual Stocks (Number of shares times their current market price per share).   _____

_____

_____

_____

Life Insurance Policy Equity This applies only to money paid into cash-value policies such as whole/variable/universal life minus commissions and fees; contact your agent if you have one.

_____

Mutual Funds Multiply the net asset value (NAV) times the number of shares you own per fund; check the business section of your newspaper for NAVs; check your fund statements for the number of shares owned. These are funds *outside of* company plans.

_____

_____

_____

_____

Qualified Retirement Plans These include 401(k)s, 403(b)s, IRAs, Keoghs, Roths, SIMPLEs, SEP-IRAs.

_____

_____

Bank Savings Accounts List CDs, interest-bearing checking accounts, passbook accounts.

_____

_____

_____

Savings/Treasury Bonds List EE Savings bonds, U.S. Treasury bonds, bills and notes.

_____

_____

_____

Other Assets

_____

_____

_____

SUBTOTAL LIQUID ASSETS   _____

Liabilities: What You Owe

Mortgage Debt (balance due)   _____

Credit-Card Debt   _____

Auto Loans (balance due)   _____

Installment Loans (lines of credit for appliances, other
items)   _____

Home-Equity Loan Debt (if applicable)   _____

Student Loans   _____

Other Debts   _____

                              SUBTOTAL LIABILITIES   _____

The Moment of Truth: Let's Do the Math

The most fundamental picture of where you stand involves some
often-painful subtraction: Liquid assets minus liabilities. Many will
come out of this equation with a negative number. If you do, don't
be alarmed. For the sake of argument and to gain a total picture of
your net worth, you can add the illiquid assets to your liquid assets.
If you still come up with a negative number, don't be discouraged.
There are a number of ways of balancing the books. We're going to
"massage" your numbers a bit more. As it turns out, you're probably owed some money by the government.

What Will Social Security Provide?

As you learned in the previous chapter, Social Security is a bit of a
chameleon these days. It'll either be carved up, downsized, or pretty
much left alone, depending on who wins the political wars in
Washington. Based on that precise forecast, how should you plan?

First, let's assume that the government will honor its promise to
provide a basic retirement benefit based on your work hours and
income. From there, we can come up with some workable numbers
based on your *Personal Earnings and Benefit Estimate Statement*

(PEBES). This is a summary of all of the money you've paid "into the system" and what your retirement benefit will be at the full retirement age of 66 or 67 (for those born after 1943 or 1960). You can, of course, take Social Security retirement payments beginning at age 63, but your monthly payments will be reduced for the rest of your life, so it's better to wait until your full retirement age to get the full payment if you can.

Summary: What Do the Numbers Mean?

You can reach a number of conclusions. If you have a positive net worth, or your assets are greater than your liabilities, you are ahead of the game. You can go straight to the chapters on investments. (who says the game Monopoly doesn't mirror life?) If you have a negative worth, you should examine which debts you can pare and which assets you can build up. If you're in this zone, read the next two chapters carefully on how to trim debt and build assets. Don't take any of these numbers too seriously, however. After all, they represent only a point in time, not a permanent condition. Remember, you can tilt the numbers in your favor.

Since there's no way of telling how much you'll need for your New Prosperity until you've decided how you want to live, the next chapter will be of some value to you. A few basic lessons will apply to everyone building their New Prosperity Plan:

1. **Pare down all debt.** Less debt means more freedom and prosperity. Pay off your mortgage if you can. Definitely pay off all your installment and credit-card debt.

> ### LATE-STARTER TIP
>
> How do you get your PEBES? Call Social Security at 800-772-1213 and ask for the PEBES request form. Fill it out (with your Social Security number and birth date of course), send it in, and in about three weeks you'll have an itemized list of years you've worked, how much you've paid into Social Security and Medicare, and how much per month you can expect at age 67. If your work records—or your personal recollection—doesn't match what Social Security has on record, document your work history and send it to Social Security. The best way to verify your work record is through check stubs or W-2s. If you were doing work for cash, however, you may be out of luck, unless your employer or person you were working for sent in FICA taxes for you.

2. **Less means more prosperity.** Cut out the things you don't need—from vacations to smoking. Make an inventory. Check your receipts.

3. **Take a realistic view of your income and assets.** If you can make more, fine, but look at what you have now. You may have substantial home equity. You may have assets that aren't working as hard as you do. In that case, you should sell off money losers or mediocre investments.

CHAPTER 3

Lifestyle Planning: Getting the Life You Want

How to Figure Out What You Need and Don't Need and an Easy Way to Save Thousands Toward Your New Prosperity Goals

"In the valley of temptation, we are all mountaineers."

When you call George Kinder at work during the winter months, you might mistake the background noise on the phone line for atmospheric interference. It sounds like waves washing up on the shore. George isn't sitting in his office in Cambridge, Massachusetts, at that time of the year. What you hear in the background isn't due to solar storms interrupting the flow of your call from the satellite. You really are hearing breakers on Maui, where George works from November until May.

George's winter work life is hardly a cliché. Although he can walk out his front door and be on the beach, he keeps in touch with all of his clients, returns phone calls, and runs much of his work through his Cambridge office. If that was all that George wanted, that would be the end of the story and we would all envy him for being a lucky stiff. As a money manager and financial planner, he goes beyond a simple handholder for wealthy clients. He wants people to understand what money means to them. Fittingly he has also discovered what money meant to him.

George is not a conventional money manager. He started out preparing taxes, but disliked that part of the business. He doesn't believe in simply chasing a rate of return or in investing only to make money. A man doesn't retreat to Maui for half the year to work without wanting more from life.

Money is a teacher and we build our maturity around it, George believes. He aims to help his clients reach their life's dreams through attaining "money maturity." He asks them some fundamental questions about how they see themselves and their money. That's before the subject of investing comes up. He finds that the more important questions have nothing to do with percentages.

"How would your life be different if you were rich?" he queries all of his clients. "How would you spend the next five years if you had all the money you needed?" Often he receives no clear answer. He has seen people trapped by their own neuroses, unable to enjoy their money. George has spent most of his career asking difficult questions of himself and his clients. The payoff is that money can be tied into peace of mind. It needn't be a disruptive force that haunts all of our waking hours. "We are trapped by our life histories and neuroses unless we develop a capacity to reach out to others to bring peace [to ourselves]," George says.

Most of us are neurotic when it comes to money. Any discussion of investing needs to begin with our past, our money history, and the nature of money itself. Even if you haven't thought of your "money personality" in forty or fifty years, now's a good time to start.

Basic Questions: Where, How, and Why

For many of our families, the first principle was that any place was better than where we came from, usually a country with a bad economy, political repression, and no chance to get ahead. The road to your New Prosperity is still quite a challenge even though our forebears have struggled to lay the groundwork for us. Nevertheless, we have choices. Starting to figure out how you want to live at midlife is a daunting task, but one that actually becomes easier with years of ruling out how you *don't* want to live. Of course nobody wants to live in an overcrowded, noisy neighborhood with lots of crime and pollution. We all want to live somewhere beautiful where we are respected for who we are and what we can contribute. Often, the question of how we want to live isn't as pressing as where. Many people in northern climates dislike winter, and as they get older their bodies become more sensitive to it, so they migrate south with the birds during the dark months.

Let's examine the "where" of your present situation. George Kinder is a great example of adjusting the where and how of his lifestyle. Having more than one residence is becoming more and more acceptable and popular. My own parents choose to live in a Chicago suburb from May to January, then head to the West Coast of Florida for the winter, where they have a condo. They decided to split their time this way when my dad retired from teaching after nearly forty years, taking an early-retirement plan he was offered. So they are close to our family in the warm months and feel the sun's warmth in the winter. But like the how of our lives, where involves some planning, too. A little courage also helps. It's not easy to uproot yourself when you're older. The decision is often based on where most of your family resides. Family is almost always the key, even if you are without a significant other or children now. You can't even ask the how and where questions, however, until you face an even more sensitive question: why? This is truly where planning for the rest of your life begins. You won't find a New Prosperity without asking this tough one and providing yourself some workable answers. Before we take on why, I'd like to relate something about my past which gives me a few whys and may help you with your queries.

We develop relationships with money at an early age. Some of our earliest impressions, of course, come from our parents. Were they rich, middle class, or poor? Was Dad working all the time? Did Mom and Dad emphasize saving or never talk about money? Did you get an allowance? What did you do with the money? An old Irish joke pokes fun at people who save at an early age: "He's so frugal, he still has his First Holy Communion money," which is given as a gift around age 8 or so. Frugality. Spendthrifts. How we see ourselves has so much to do with our childhood that we are often captive of these early attitudes and feelings.

My Own Story

My first recollection of my relationship with money came during the summer of 1967. It was the "Summer of Love," although I was too young to appreciate what that meant. The Beatles had changed recording history with *St. Pepper's Lonely Hearts Club Band,* but my three brothers and I were not allowed to listen to the album; my music-teacher father objected to John Lennon's comment that the Beatles were "bigger than Jesus." Like many of his peers, my father, who was a Big Band musician, didn't think too much of rock music.

At the time, civil rights and urban unrest were tearing cities apart, especially on the West and South Sides of Chicago. I believe my dad tried to take his mind off the war and turmoil in the country that year by building an addition to the house. Besides, we needed the room. He was constructing while the country was deconstructing.

We lived thirty-five miles south of the city in a nearly all-white suburb (the near opposite is true today). In 1967, our fifties tract house had begun to feel small as we matured. At the time, it had two bedrooms, one small bathroom, a basement, and a one-car garage. The attic had been partially converted to a bedroom for my brother Steve and me. As we got older, though, the one pizza that used to feed us on Sunday expanded to two, then three as our appetites and bodies grew. Back then, a pizza came with either sausage or pepperoni and cheese, was as thin as a printed-circuit board, and cost just a few dollars. Gasoline was about 60¢ a gallon. You could buy a commodious sedan for $2,000. Utilities, health care, and housing costs hadn't entered the inflationary, post-Vietnam spiral of the 1970s and '80s. McDonald's was only one of thousands of drive-ins, and such food was considered a luxury for a growing family. Mom mostly cooked simple things that boys like: hamburgers, hot dogs, spaghetti, lots of mashed potatoes, and macaroni and cheese.

Since my father was a teacher, he was off from June until late August. Usually he taught summer school for the extra money. In 1967, however, he decided he could save hundreds by building an addition that would include a half-bath, another bedroom, and a family room. He had worked summers with my uncle Russ on construction crews, so he knew basic carpentry. All he needed was someone to pour the foundation and put in some ceiling tile. The rest was his domain. I think that we were enlisted to help him with this project at first, then were ushered off to the backyard by my mom when our assistance exceeded its usefulness.

The summers then hung like a slack clothesline in the stifling Midwestern heat. They just limped through until the first frost came, which were always too soon or too late, depending on how your summer went and if you were getting any decent teachers that year in school (for some reason, I always developed crushes on the ladies that were sternest with me). That summer was taut with ideas, things I had never contemplated as the world came apart outside of our suburban enclave. First, there was the matter of the siding Dad ripped off the back of the house. It was cedar painted white. Back then, every frame house was sided with cedar painted white. Every house on the block of the subdivision looked the same. It was this sameness that made America tolerable for some and maddening for others. White, middle-class America was symbolized by the White House with the white bread in the kitchen, white communion wafers in church, and white gloves for the ladies during formal events. The country was run by a white guy in a white house who coincidentally liked white shoes. It always surprised me that the currency wasn't white. I wouldn't even meet an Asian- or African-American until I was in my teens.

The siding from our house became the exterior of a clubhouse I built with my brothers. A horizontal steel tube that had been the main support for our swing set, now unused owing to our mobility on bikes, became the center beam for the roof. Actually, it was more of a lean-to that faced south, with the planks of siding covering the north face. The front of the structure was open with a counter. Although I had no intention of designing it thus, it was suitable for a retail business. I think my mom suggested that we pursue the fine art of shoe-shining in a time when almost all men's shoes, except for the guys at the Country Club, were black. Of course there were brown shoes, but those were the exception, not the rule.

Mrs. Rosetti, our backyard neighbor, saw our efforts and paid us a visit to give us her advice on how to "spit shine" shoes. When she was a B-girl during World War II, this was one of her duties, which she relished because she got to meet GIs. With Mrs. Rosetti's advice, we corraled some neighbor-clients and were in business. Since our labor was free and our capital consisted of two cans of Kiwi shoe polish, a few rags, and a polishing brush, our operating expenses were low. There was no rent and our labor and spit were limitless.

The money was heavenly. I think we charged 50¢ a pair, which might as well have been $50 at the time. From that venture, we expanded. My mom thought we should do a newsletter chronicling the events of the summer on the block. My dad had an old mimeograph machine that the school had discarded, so all we needed was paper and mimeograph fluid. This was pre–desktop publishing, so we typed the newsletter directly onto a master, which could be reproduced several thousand times. We charged a quarter for this publication, which was well received. We dubbed it the *216th Place Journal.* My mom, a high school newspaper editor, probably had more fun than we did. Our activities made those sultry summer days without a swimming pool go by quickly. It also showed me that creativity could be compensated, no doubt influencing my choice of profession. I saved my money, probably for some worthless faux Indian tomahawk I would buy on our next vacation into the Rockies, Utah, and Arizona the following summer. My brother Tom was the real frugal one, never spending his money on vacation and usually borrowing (from us) to buy his trinkets.

That summer tied money, saving, and time together into this quilt of experience for me. The money was important *because* of the time. We all have memories that not only define our childhoods but are signposts for values we will have forever. Our regard for money is tied into how our parents saw it, how we came to appreciate it, and what it did for us in our child's eye. Because of my pleasant summers, I always tied money into vacations, the freedom to start new things, and the need to preserve those carefree days of productive indolence. I will never have the time back again, but the experience I gained from it has some value and immutable symbolism. I want to save money the way I want to save summers. Money comes and goes like a thousand summer sunsets. It simply buys you a better present and future. Like a memory, it's both symbolic and dynamic. How we define it shapes our lives in a thousand, table-spooned-sized ways.

Money as a Symbol

No doubt you've gone into a coffee shop and seen a dollar bill or two taped to the inside of the counter, the proverbial "first dollar" the owner made in the business. Or you've seen coins converted into necklaces. Or how about the prolific use of the icons on money?

Let's start with the anatomy of a dollar bill. In a clever use of symbolism designed by the government to ensure faith in the quality of its debt, the creators of the dollar bill tied in God, his/her approval of the American Republic, and the sanctity of the U.S. Treasury. Talk about mixing metaphors. It's purely intentional. If people had no faith in the institution behind the money—in this case a Federal Reserve note for legal tender—there would be unbelievable inflation or anarchy. The most interesting symbol on the dollar bill is the pyramid with the eye on top. The motto *Annuit Coeptis Norvus Ordo Seclorum* roughly means "he has approved our undertaking, a new order of the ages." Who's *he?* George Washington? Thomas Jefferson? Alan Greenspan? No. The eye is meant to be God's. Although the United States is a secular state with no state religion, the founding fathers believed that the divinity approved of their efforts, looking down upon the pyramid as a symbol of a solidly built republic. Notice no mention of faith, democracy, capitalism, plurality, the Congress, or the Supreme Court. Just "In God We Trust," the pyramid, and the usual government monuments.

Also note that there is no mention on the bill of "the pursuit of happiness" or any other line from the Declaration of Independence or Constitution. So there's no *guarantee* that God smiling down on the Republic will provide happiness or material sustenance. What's left? The pyramid is also said to be the symbol of freemasonry, a quasi-religious group that combines the tenets of Christianity, Plato, Pythagoras, and sound construction techniques. Masons used their devotion to God and their obedience to the rules of geometry to build everything from Gothic cathedrals to structures such as the U.S. Capitol, the Smithsonian Institution, and the Washington Monument. What underpins this connection between God, architecture, and the state? Faith. Trust. But are we putting faith in the currency itself or the institutions behind it? If the dollar was backed by gold or something precious and tangible, we would be asked to have faith that there were enough gold bars in Fort Knox to back up the more than $5 trillion in the national debt plus all the currency outstanding at any given time. The gold standard, however, was phased out nearly thirty years ago. Forget about silver, platinum, palladium, or even hamburgers backing the bucks out there. There's simply not enough of any of these things in the possession of the U.S. Treasury. The government is asking you to accept its promise of "full faith and credit" at face value. What kind of promise is that?

The symbols on the U.S. currency tell the story: government buildings, ancient structures, the eye of the deity; slogans that tell us of the deity's approval of the new world order, whatever that is. In the larger sense, money symbolizes our hopes and dreams, our sweat and our trust in the infinite creativity of human nature—hence the new world order. From this, prosperity is ensured through a political compact and sealed by a divine sanction that is built on trust. Those who declare that money is godless or evil could not be more wrong. Money symbolizes our highest aspirations. As Tad Crawford explains in his illuminating *Secret Life of Money:*

> No wonder "In God We Trust" appears on all of our coins and bills. In times of recession or depression, this slogan offers a way to understand why money fails us. Money, although a secular tool, requires our trust in the richness of a divine power. If we feel a constriction in the flow of money-blood, then we will yearn for more life energy. If we feel that our political leaders are sacrificing

us, then we (living in a democracy and not a theocracy) will demand their sacrifice.[1]

Crawford introduces several concepts that are important to our understanding of money. There's *money-blood,* which refers to the material fluid that sustains our everyday lives. *Life energy* is the power that makes money-blood flow, or our ability to work and make a living at something. Sacrifice, that most ancient of concepts, is that which we must forgo to convert our life energy into money so that we can be sustained. All of this is built on faith in government, the government's social compact, and some divine supervision. In a working democracy, the government is *us.* We are the government because we elect others to represent us. Ultimately, our trust is in *ourselves.*

Before the American and French revolutions, our ancestors were asked to trust their sovereigns, who proclaimed *their* powers came directly from God. When the powers of the enlightened, beneficent state replaced those of pharaohs, emperors, the Imperial Republic, the church, kings, queens, tsars, despots, and dictators, the conduct of our affairs was placed in our hands. Money fits neatly in your hands. Your hands, heart, and mind shape the creation of it. It's an abstract concept that goes back to Plato by way of Shakespeare: "to thine own self be true." Trust yourself and money will become the pyramid of your existence, cemented by the divine architect.

Money goes beyond symbolism, however, because it's also a powerful medium of exchange. It opens doors and buys houses. It greases the wheels of commerce, politics, and every other social institution. Philosopher Jacob Needleman, in his revealing *Money and the Meaning of Life,* explains the depth of the power money has over us:

Like technology—and money is a form of technology—money is good at solving problems; it is bad at opening questions. Like technology, money is used wrongly when it converts inner questions that should be lived into problems to be solved. Money fixes things, but not every difficulty in life should be fixed.[2]

Money and the Family

Plotting out your future with money, even if you haven't examined your relationship with it over the past four or five decades, is not going to be easy if you don't know what you believe in when it comes to currency. This is the how and where of money. How can you possibly think of retirement unless you have some idea of what money has meant to you and how it has shaped your life? How can you take a driving vacation unless you know where you're starting and where you're going? Wouldn't a map help?

This is a subjective survey of your money geography. We're drawing a word map. I suggest you answer each question carefully in a quiet place with no distractions from family or electronic devices. Don't even think about sitting near a phone, radio, VCR, pager, or clock. Put your cell phone in your car unless the only quiet place you know of *is* your car. Looking out the window or taking a long walk is highly recommended.

The Geography of Money: Mapping Where You've Been

BEGIN YOUR JOURNEY: EARLIEST PLACES OF MONEY MEMORY
Place yourself in the location where you first learned about money. Was it in your family home? A relative's home? A bank? Your place of worship dropping money in a basket? Where did your money go? What did it do? Did you get an allowance? Did it give you a sense of control? Freedom? Guilt? Shame? Autonomy? Identity?

SACRED MONEY PLACES. WHERE WERE THEY?
Picture the places where money held a special place. Was there a special room in your home where it was discussed? Did your parents take you with them to the bank? Did you have a piggy bank in your bedroom? Where did you store your money? Did you have a savings account? What did you save for? What happened when you didn't have enough money to get what you wanted? What did you do with money from birthdays and other special events? Did you get savings bonds, coins, or cash? Did you spend it right away or save for something special? Did you give to charity at an early age?

MONEY DURING YOUR SCHOOL DAYS

Did you spend your lunch money on something other than lunch or milk? What did you do with it if you saved it? Where did you spend this extra money? Did you buy your own school supplies? Did you buy a special lunch box? Did you feel you had enough money during school? Did other kids have more money and make you feel guilty you had less or vice versa? Where were you when you felt shame over money? Did you have a car in high school? Did you pay for the expenses associated with owning and maintaining it or did your parents cover all the costs? Where did you go in your car (if you had access to it)? Did you save for college? Did you get a scholarship or loans? How much did debt burden you when you left? Where were you when you finished high school or college? Were you in debt? Who in your family taught you about money (if anyone)? Where were you when you first learned about it?

YOUNG ADULTHOOD: THE GEOGRAPHY OF THE RECENT PAST

Where was your first job? How much did it pay? Did you live on your own immediately after graduation (from high school or college)? How much did your rent cost? Where was your apartment or home then? Did you marry early? Where did your marriage take place? How much did it cost? Did you pay for some or all of it? When did you buy your first home? Where was (is) it? Where do you work now? Is it enough to make ends meet?

WHERE YOU ARE NOW

Where do you work and live? Is it where you want to be? Has your money path led you in the direction you wanted to take (if you had a direction)?

WHERE YOU WANT TO BE

Where is it you want to be? Are you there yet? How do you want to get there?

Money Geography 101: Do You Know Where You Are?

The purpose of this money mapping is to show you where your money route has taken you. This is what you should ask yourself about your destinations:

1. Has it led you into a canyon of debt and self-doubt?

2. Has it purchased you the place (house, neighborhood, town) where you think you want to stay for the next thirty years or so?

3. Has it led you to a place where you needn't connect your identity, place in society, or ego with how much you have? In this place, money is of little importance.

4. Has it led you to a place where you feel uncomfortable with yourself?

5. If the lack of money is a problem, do you need to change the route and destination?

If you answered yes to questions 1, 4, or 5, move on to the next section. If you answered yes to questions 2 and/or 3, move on to the next chapter.

Money Addictions: Do You Have a Problem?

Chances are, you've had your fair share of pop psychology, group therapy, and feel-good drugs (tranquilizers, nicotine, alcohol, antidepressants). So I won't burden you with a needs assessment to identify any deep-rooted psychopathologies. We've been overzenned, Oprahed, Donohued, and Prozaced over the past thirty years or so. You might already have discovered that it's really difficult to change. For most of us, money wasn't at the root of every problem, but our shortcomings certainly influenced our dealings with money. It's well known that marriages, friendships, and businesses dissolve over differences concerning money. There are groups to counsel people who spend money they don't have (Debtors Anonymous), people who gamble too much (Gamblers Anonymous), and drink too much (Alcoholics Anonymous).

You're probably familiar with the list of what Anne Wilson Schaef calls process addictions:

- Sex

- Eating

- Work

- Excitement

- Substance abuse

- Gambling

- Abuse

- Hypochondriasis

- Religion

- Money

- Power

- Tragedy

- Entertainment

Add to that established list new maladies centered around abuse of information and technology:

- Television

- Video games

- Cell phones and pagers

- The Internet

- The cult of celebrity

- Driving

- Audio/videophilia

- Computing

Each addiction or abusive behavior is based on the illusion that the activity will satisfy, prolong, delay, or defuse some inner need we have. Coincidentally, each one can be purchased with money, so money becomes a conduit to an undesirable activity—if it is practiced in excess. But many people wrongly identify the core problem as something to do with money: not having enough of it, overspending it, or having too much. You can be rich, middle class, or poor and still enjoy your life. Money merely channels our energy.

So what do we need that money really can't buy? In a world of limitless information that's accessible at any time or place, there are still human longings and basic components of personality development that can be short-circuited. Psychologists Abraham Maslow and Erik Erikson charted these needs earlier in the century. A brief summary of these needs and my interpretation of them include:

I. **Truth, goodness, and beauty.** If we are deprived of these qualities, "metapathologies" emerge that range from distrust to cynicism.

II. **Unity/wholeness/dichotomy/transcendence.** If we can't recognize our connectedness to our behaviors and the world, we tend to see everything as a duel or war, resulting in a continuous conflict with life.

III. **Aliveness, process, uniqueness.** If we don't feel alive and special, we lose a feeling of self, resulting in chronic boredom and a sense of deadness.

IV. **Perfection, necessity, completion/finality.** We need to find purpose in life's projects. Otherwise we feel that life is chaotic and there's no use trying.

V. **Justice and order.** Security and safety are essential to well-being.

VI. **Simplicity, richness, totality.** Life is complicated, but we need to see things with clarity and depth and have some notion of the big picture.

VII. **Effortlessness, playfulness.** We have to enjoy life and have a sense of humor about things. It's a key to survival.

VIII. **Self-sufficiency, meaningfulness.** We have to stand on our own and see some purpose in what we're doing.[3]

Dr. Erikson called these human attributes "B-Values"; he believed that each one "enhances or fulfills the human potential."[4] Without them guiding our lives, we fall prey to the process addictions, which lead to messy lives and a profound disconnection from our environment and society. As animals cast adrift in a world full of temptations (food, booze, sex, information), we find it all too easy to lose our bearings. Our base instincts take over and we eat, drink, and abuse ourselves to death. Our higher selves are neglected.

Erikson further observed in his classic *Childhood and Society* that "the metapathologies of the affluent and indulged young [you're not old yet] come partly from deprivation of intrinsic values, frustrated 'idealism' from disillusionment with a society that they see (mistakenly) motivated only by lower or animal or material needs."[5]

There's a powerful reason why Erikson finishes that revealing statement with material needs and connects them with lower or animal needs. In the puritanical thinking that has so dominated the Anglo-American global economy, money has been depicted as dirty—that is, unclean. The biblical phrase "the *love* of money is the root of all evil" has become truncated over time to "money is the root of all evil," which isn't true. Money itself is not the source of evil, but the toll our desire for it has on our moral and spiritual character.

Personal Money Ecology: Reprogramming Your Money Energy Flow

Assuming that you have this disconnect between the purpose of money and how it flows into or out of your life, let's revisit some definitions. It's never too late to revise your attitudes. This is another sit-by-yourself, turn-off-the-world kind of exercise, designed to show you not only what your relationship to money is, but how you can change it if it's out of balance. That's where your "personal ecology" comes in. You're trying to find a natural balance between your needs and the needs of those around you. There are no outside goals or standards of living that you must conform to in order to be in balance. What feels right? Where do you want to be? You have to determine your own needs. What's throwing you out of sync with where you need to be? Ecology is about relationships.

Again, this is purely subjective. Your answers in this exercise will mirror how you feel about this important subject. Don't worry, since you won't be compared to "the norm," "a national average," or "the standard." This is where modern social science research fails us anyway. There are no meaningful standards when it comes to how we view ourselves, our families, and our economic situations. We're all different because we have different needs based on how we were raised, our current status, and our definition of the New Prosperity. Everyone's family life is qualitatively different.

I suggest you photocopy this section and check the appropriate column and then put your answers away for a week. Then pull them out and read each answer aloud. Justify your answers. You'll be surprised how revealing your answers to these questions can be. Remember, there is no set of right or wrong answers and no grading key.

A. THE ROLE MONEY PLAYS IN LIFE

Agree Disagree

Money is for paying for things pure and simple.

You can live without love, but not without money.

Having money isn't the same thing as wealth.

If I'm bored, money always fixes the problem.

Money is energy, allowing life to flow.

I work only for the money.

I have debts because I don't have enough money.

Spending money is more important than saving.

I'll never afford a comfortable retirement.

I'm optimistic that I can earn more money.

I feel guilty about how much money I make.

I spend within my means.

Agree Disagree

Earning money also gives me knowledge.

I save every penny, but where does it get me?

Work is an instrument of life.

The more money I make, the better I feel.

I can never get the numbers to add up every month.

My credit card is a ticket to happiness.

Prosperity is only partially related to earnings.

My vitality is connected with making money.

B. DEFINING WEALTH AND PROSPERITY

Agree Disagree

Spending time with my family is more
   important than working long hours
   and making more money.

I like the quality of my life now.

I would give up things to enjoy my life more.

Wealth means you have everything you want.

To have prosperity, you must be greedy.

I'll never be prosperous with the job I have.

Religion plays a role in my money attitudes.

I'm deluded when it comes to spending money.

The wealthiest people have the most time.

My family has always been mad about money.

Wealth is like sex, you can never have too much.

Agree   Disagree

Prosperity means not taking money too seriously.

I'll never be wealthy because I can't take control.

Wealth is a negative in life.

Wealth is a positive in life.

I'm in denial over my obsession with money.

My spouse/significant other is obsessed about
wealth to the point that it is ruining our
relationship.

I'm constantly focused on becoming wealthy.

All I've ever wanted was to be wealthy.

Prosperity is a good family life.

Your Personal Money Ecology

You've just taken a kind of essay test. The best part is that you didn't
actually have to write an essay and there's no scoring or even right
or wrong answers. You will not be compared to anyone else and no
one else has to know how you responded. You certainly don't have
to send in your answers to me, a university, or any federal agency.
You will not be put on a mailing list or compared to a national average. Besides, there is no national average for this exercise. Your
answers are for your own personal reflection. They will give you
some guidance concerning what you need to examine to reach a
healthy relationship with money. If you want some guideposts as to
how you might regard your responses, here are some ideas.

- **Money *is* connected to our vitality.** How we make it, spend it, or
  invest it flows in and out of our lives. It is not at the core of our
  lives, however. Money is simply this river of energy that connects
  work, our livelihoods (not always work), and our family/home
  life with the rest of the world. Money is a living force created by
  hearts, minds, and bodies. Ever try to rip up a dollar bill? Did

you ever wonder why such as simple act is so difficult? You can't do it, can you? It symbolizes blood, sweat, and tears, to paraphrase Churchill. We don't live to make money, but money does facilitate our living.

- **Money is not prosperity, nor is it wealth.** Prosperity and wealth are two different ideas. *Prosperity* refers to hope, fortune, and flourishing in life. *Webster's New World College Dictionary* gives the modern definition as "to succeed, thrive, grow, etc. in a vigorous way." Hence the connection with vitality. There's an intimate connection with the business of living here. *Wealth* concerns an amount of worldly possessions, according to *Webster's New World*. Wealth is an economic measurement of tangible things. One other definition is well-being, which is spiritual and physical in nature, closer to the Old Saxon word related to *will* or a "sound and prosperous state." Wealth is the evolved concept of the human determination to be in a well state. We become wealthy because we acquire things, but all too often we define ourselves by those things. The more useful definition is to define ourselves by our well-being. Can you have wealth and prosperity without well-being and hope? Of course not.

- **Wealth is positive and negative, but prosperity is always positive.** You can have too many things in life. They can overwhelm you. Prosperity is more often shared as a function of family and social life. The Roman Empire was wealthy, but not necessarily prosperous. Romans owned slaves and those who lived outside Rome didn't have the fine sewers, water system, public baths, or food supply that the Romans had built for their free citizens. Periclean Athens was a prosperous state as well, but it also thrived with the help of slaves. The United States shares its wealth and is in many ways prosperous, but that prosperity is not shared by everyone. The well-being that is an intimate partner of prosperity is not shared by those plagued by disease, drugs, poverty, or violence. The ideal is to enhance well-being by choosing prosperity over just acquiring money or material goods. Ironically, you can be very wealthy but not prosperous.

- There's a close connection between money, sex, religion, work, relationships, family, and society. You'll have to define your relationships for yourself. All of the statements you agreed with indicating your relationship with these subjects give you a framework for your money ecology. You can tell from your agreements or disagreements where you stand and what may be out of balance. Does your work disrupt your sense of well-being? If so, you might look for another job or line of work. You can't save aggressively for retirement if you need to work longer and won't find the intervening years worthwhile. If you are working to support one of the various addictions, then you also need to reprogram your need for them. What are you working for? If it's just for the money, then you will have a hard time defining your own New Prosperity.

Document What You Want Now

You'll need some specific goals after isolating what you want and what you don't want. Document them now by writing them down:

What I want for myself_____

_____

What I want for my significant other or family_____

_____

What I need (i.e., better job, better health care, etc.)_____

_____

What I need for my significant other or family_____

_____

What I don't need (what's out of balance)_____

_____

Lynne Twist, who works with the Hunger Project and produces "The Soul of Money" workshops for the Institute of Noetic Sciences in Sausalito, California, has a workable definition of wealth and prosperity worth keeping in mind:

Wealth to me—and another word we might use is prosperity—is a sense of joy and creativity and fulfillment in life. And, you know, people have that, but they don't label it wealth. Every morning the sun comes up and lights up the sky, no matter where you live. And when you sit and watch the sunset, you realize the wealth, prosperity, and well-being that's available to you just in the relationship with the earth, with the sun, with the solar system we're in, and the stars. Wealth is understanding the beauty and magnificence of a tree. Wealth is being in love with your husband, in love with your wife, in love with your work. Wealth is having the joy of raising a child. This is wealth, in my book, and those things don't cost anything. They are an investment of the human spirit. And when our human spirit is unleashed, what's unleashed is the prosperity of the soul, the prosperity of the heart, an experience of love, relatedness, and the deep truth that we are each other. And in that truth, the whole world belongs to you.[6]

Self-Ethics and the Myth of Consumption: What's Keeping You from Prosperity

If you choose to redefine your money ecology, then change is possible and you can attain that New Prosperity. You may already be on the path to "right livelihood," which is an ecological way of living. Dottie Koontz, a financial planner in Seattle, offers even more insights on money ecology: "Money is a resource. It helps us do what we want to do. It's an efficient way of exchanging energy. We're [all too often] money's servant; *it* drives us. I think people are waking up and finding that there's something more. We're reclaiming our souls."[7] Koontz recalls a trip she took to Egypt where she rode horseback through a village and discovered that people were in the street just talking to each other after ten at night, a time when most Americans are watching the evening news on television. It amazed her that people could "just be out talking," a simple act uncommon in our society today. Let's look at some ways in which to turn your reflective monologue on personal ecology into a plan for the New Prosperity.

Part of the promise of the New Prosperity is that you develop a means to achieve it, even if you are starting late. To keep on track, you'll need to monitor yourself to ensure that you are conforming to your "needs and wants" statements.

You've been brutally honest with yourself up until this point and outlined what you want and don't want and some roadblocks to what you need. Let's move outside of your personal ecology and look at how the outside world may be working against your attaining your New Prosperity.

Uncontrolled Spending and Your New Prosperity

One of the most plausible explanations social scientists offer for our inability to create a harmonious personal ecology is the constant assault of commerce. It's now possible to be pitched a product or service every hour of the day in nearly any location in the United States. We're exposed to marketing and advertising everywhere we turn: expressway billboards driving to work, radio and television, sports venues, doctor's/dentist's offices, children's videos, and the Internet. With the advent of satellite television and the Internet, we are marketed to twenty-four hours a day from every conceivable vendor on the planet. The message is relentless: *Spend your money.*

While the consumer economy keeps people employed, keeps money flowing in the economy, and is the lifeblood of a free market, it is built on convincing people that they need a product or service that (ninety-nine times out of a hundred) they can live without. What's being advertised rarely contributes to our prosperity. The opposite is true. It sucks money out of our lives by deceiving us into thinking that we will be younger, sexier, more beautiful, and more popular if we buy that product. Most sales pitches are based on the assumption that we see ourselves as inadequate, ugly, lonely, stupid, unpopular, overweight, aging, and incompetent. Such insecurities are common to every human being. Advertising relays the myth that by buying products, we become somebody better. Most of this is familiar territory covered masterfully by writers such as Vance Packard and Marshall McLuhan. As a result of a "shop until you drop" mentality, we don't save or invest for the future.

Some of the best research on the effects of marketing and advertising on our well-being has come from the Washington-based Center for the Study of Commercialism. In their classic *Marketing Madness: A Survival Guide for a Consumer Society,* Michael Jacobson and Laurie Ann Mazur provide frightening details concerning how commerce invades, perverts, subverts, and all too often rules our lives. Even if you are just starting to think about money and an easier life, you may not be aware of the degree that commercialism has upended society and your own life. Jacobson and Mazur examine marketing to children, infomercials, fake news stories that are really advertising, sexism, environmental impacts, and the undermining of every social institution. The net result: loss of community and lack of any sense of saving for the future. Here's how Jacobson and Mazur see it:

> The tidal wave of advertising messages drowns out the few countervailing calls to be frugal or save for a costly crisis. Other than the occasional ads from financial institutions, we are almost never urged to save or invest our money for our family's or our nation's future. The result, not surprisingly, is a society that lives for the moment and is ill-prepared for financial crisis.[8]

There's a great deal of evidence to suggest that the persistent siren call of advertising is creating second-by-second barriers to our own prosperity. So here's the first and most basic New Prosperity Principle: *You can't save or invest if you are constantly spending money (often money you don't have) for things you don't need and can't afford.* The easy availability of credit and "no/low down payment" vehicle leasing are two ways into this trap. The following are some other examples:

- Easy credit means easy debt. By the end of 1996, a record 1.1 million Americans filed for personal bankruptcy, up 28.6% from 1995 and up 44.1% from 1994, according to *The Economist.* The average finance charge on this debt: 15.8%. At a time when banks were paying you a paltry 4% to 5% on savings instruments, savings institutions had a vested interest in making profits from debt.[9]

- Brand advertising has invaded every type of product category. Disney characters are on everything from children's bedsheets to underwear. Licensed apparel is designed to lock you into a brand for life, ensuring that you will pay inflated prices and advertise a company's product to boot. Brand advertising increases the price of a product that is not better than a generic product. "It is consumers who end up paying for the nearly $150 billion—or almost $600 per person—that companies spend on advertising," Jacobson and Mazur found. "For instance, when we buy cosmetics, compact discs, and games, 10% or more of the price goes for promotional costs."[10]

- Advertising steals our time (when we watch television, movies, videos, the Internet) and tells us lies (we'll have more friends, be sexier, more beautiful, etc.). While telling us lies, it slowly kills us by selling us tobacco, fat/cholesterol-laden foods, and unhealthy lifestyles (look at nearly every beer ad).

- Advertising tells us that all new technology is good, sex sells, and shopping is a worthwhile activity. It also exploits our love for our families (bring the kids to a theme park or fast-food restaurant instead of to a park and for a family cookout).

- Television, the greatest selling medium ever invented, is the source of the whale's share of advertising beamed directly into our living rooms, bedrooms, and children's minds. The average U.S. family has two television sets and leaves the tube on for six hours, forty-seven minutes a day. That totals 250 *billion* hours watched annually by Americans, according to studies by the A. C. Nielsen Company. What do we get when we watch this much television? The average child will see 20,000 commercials per year (2 million by age 65) and 200,000 violent acts (by age 18) and will waste 1,500 hours per year watching television (versus 900 hours in school).[11] As a result, studies have linked television watching to obesity, heart/lung disease, retarded social skills, and an increased incidence of violent behavior. Dr. Robert Putnam, a Harvard political scientist, even found that "TV viewing is strongly and negatively related to social trust and group membership; the more people watch, the less they are engaged with others."[12]

- Advertising, which is an unabashed cheerleader for unbridled consumption, is harming our communities and planet. It encourages expensive, nonlocally made, disposable items and packaging. Pollution is created, landfills are filling up, and energy is used to transport and dispose of it all. The packaging industry alone creates 200 billion bottles, cans, and containers every year, all of it disposable (and only a minuscule percentage is recycled). According to Alan Thein Durning, an environmental consumption expert and author of *How Much Is Enough?*, "if the life-supporting ecosystems of the world are to survive for future generations, the consumer society will have to dramatically curtail its use of resources—partly by shifting to high-quality, low-input durable goods and partly by seeking fulfillment through leisure, human relationships, and other nonmaterial avenues."[13]

The bottom line isn't that advertising or consumption is bad. Unfortunately, advertising does tell us that we are basically incomplete and inadequate while prosperity is around the corner. Western marketing also sells us snake-oil solutions. It's too easy to say that turning off your television and ignoring advertising will help you save money. You've known that all of your life. Since advertising is now omnipresent from the Gobi Desert to Georgia, there are too many subtle—and not so subtle—messages being hurled at your brain (some 3,000 per day, according to *Business Week*) every day. That's why you'll need to take another walk in the park to contemplate the next section.

Coming Down from the Mountain: A Lifestyle You Can Live With *Now*

Nearly a decade ago, my wife Kathleen and I visited her native Ireland. For her, it was a homecoming and a chance to show off the "big Yank" (me). She grew up in West Belfast dodging the British Army, the Irish Republican Army, and the maw of poverty. It was a traumatic return for her because her life in the United States was so different, so full of possibilities—an unsettling contrast to the culture of despair that permeated her Catholic neighborhood, where high unemployment forced nearly everyone onto welfare in some way. People lived in constant tension, drank and smoke too much, and worried about assaults from the IRA, the police, or various Protestant extremist groups. Kathleen's mother, Theresa, who would later start and run a successful drapery business in Chicago, was a victim of one of the IRA bombings. They pulled her out of the rubble of a building that had been blown up. She was on tranquilizers for years after that.

I couldn't sleep at night when I stayed in Kathleen's aunt's Belfast home. The noises that you hear at night consisted of police helicopters, screaming, and cars peeling away. Although a beautiful city, it was hardly a tourist destination then. The South Bronx seemed like a paradise by comparison. Kathleen had no intention of going back there to live, although most of her family still live there and they are attempting to lead normal lives. A lifestyle in West Belfast consisted mostly of working (if you could find a decent job), smoking, drinking, and trying to stay alive. After a week of seeing every relative of Kathleen's, we headed to the West Coast of Ireland.

Letting go of our angst on the exquisite coast in Counties Clare and Mayo, we seized upon the idea of one day moving there (we do that during every relaxing vacation). Ireland is one of the Western world's best-kept secrets. It's not overcommercialized; the people are gracious and friendly; and there are places where there are no billboards, no luxury condos, no theme parks, and no advertising whatsoever save for the occasional Guinness or Bass sign on the local pub. Before we settled into a bed and breakfast in a town called Lahinch, we had literally climbed a mountain. This mountain was not tall, only about a half-mile high, but it was special: St. Patrick's *Croagh Patrick*. National legend has it that the saint himself spent forty days and forty nights on the summit to contemplate how to convert the then-pagan Irish.

The first quarter-mile up the mountain was a gradual incline. Then the path narrowed and the grade steepened. When we got to the halfway point, we discovered the commodes placed there for the convenience of pilgrims: a concrete lean-to facing north with a hole in the ground. From there, the route to the summit was difficult. There was no path, simply millions of sharp-edged rocks at oblique angles that you had to crawl on one at a time. A fellow from Boston I met at the halfway point was climbing *barefoot* up the mountain. I asked him why he was subjecting his feet to the torture. "I have a lot of sins" was his reply as he walked on in pain.

Kathleen was wearing some cheap flats perfectly unsuited for climbing. I asked her several times if she wanted to turn back. She refused, despite her discomfort. The wind started to howl across Clew Bay to the point that we could barely stand up. It was a warm wind, however, as Ireland was experiencing record heat. The skies looked like a welterweight's eyes after a punishing bout.

After nearly three hours, we made it to the top. There was a tiny chapel there, but the door was locked. The wind tossed Kathleen's hair around as if she were on a ship in the middle of the Atlantic, which we could see miles to the west dotted by an archipelago of un-inhabited islands in the quiet inlet of the bay. I expected to have a revelation there, a spiritual experience that would transform the rest of my life. I wanted it to be like the last two minutes of a close bas-ketball game in which Michael Jordan swishes in an off-balance shot. Nothing like that happened, though. After all, thousands of pilgrims had climbed the mountain, typically at night with a candle in hand, often barefoot. The sick would be carted up in stretchers for the saint's blessing. There was a slot in the white statue of the saint for alms. That was the only connection with money. There were no gift shops, vending machines, or T-shirt kiosks. The summit was just as pristine. My spiritual experience was a sense of warm emptiness. You couldn't see a single telephone pole, television aerial, billboard, or radio antenna from the summit. All I could see was sky, ocean, and the triangular mountains that stretched north along the untamed coastline. It was magnificent for the fullness of the experience—and my puniness in the face of it. I realized why we needed to be remote from our material lives once and a while. Emptiness was fullness. It didn't need to be entertaining. Other than the plane fare and lodging expenses on the Emerald Isle, climbing the mountain cost me nothing. It asked nothing of me but gave me things I could not buy.

Living with material needs and desires often means living with things that clutter your life with empty promises, false visions, and pleasures you don't even desire. It's so difficult to design your plan for New Prosperity with four or more decades of advertising images in your head telling you what you should buy, consume, and *be*.

The beauty of living without is that some of the following items you probably won't miss once you don't have them anymore. This will free up your mind for reflecting on what you really want to do and how you want to get there.

Living in the Material World: An Amenities Audit of Must-Haves and Don't-Needs

If you must have something, there's no real argument. But if you're really honest, you don't need some of the following. Check the appropriate spaces in this partial "amenities audit." Add to the list anything I've forgotten. Use the approximate savings to funnel into your New Prosperity investments you will craft in the next several chapters.

Item	Must Have	Don't Need	Could Save
Television (in 98% of U.S. households)			$100–$4,000
Radio (same %)			$10–$500
Phone (96% of households, cordless not included)			$20–$100
Videocassette player/ recorder (89% of homes)			$100–$1,000
Cordless phone (66% of homes, not always private)			$50–$150
Telephone answering machine (65%)			$25–$100

Item	Must Have	Don't Need	Could Save
Stereo system (54%)			$75+
Compact disc player (49%)			$75–$1,000
Personal computer (40%)			$500–$3,000
Computer printer (38%)			$150–$2,000
Cellular phone (34%)			$10+
Pager (28%)			$10+
Vehicle alarm (27%)			$100–$2,000
Camcorder (26%)			$250–$2,000
Computer with CD-ROM (21%)			$1,500–$3,000
Direct-view satellite service (10%)			$500+
Fax machine (9%)			$100–$500
Cable television service			$500–$1,000
Internet access service			$120+
Microwave oven			$50–$250
Other			

Major Temptations

Item	Must Have	Don't Need	Could Save
Second vehicle ($20,000 nominal cost/leased)			$3,600/yr.
(Add maintenance, fuel, insurance, licenses)			$2,500/yr.+
Powerboat (small)			$2,000+

Item	Must Have	Don't Need	Could Save
(Add storage, fuel, maintenance, trailer, license)			$1,500+
Overseas vacation (two weeks in London or Paris)			$3,000+
Second home (you name the place and price)			?

NOTE: Estimates for the major temptations are mine. You can spend much, much more depending on what you buy. Where there is a plus sign, you can spend an unlimited amount of money. For all electronic items, the source is the Consumer Electronics Manufacturers Association for January 1997.

ANOTHER THING YOU COULD LIVE WITHOUT

SAVE BIG ... Amazing! You could save up to $86,000 by giving up your weekly lottery tickets for twenty years and investing that money in your 401(k) instead.

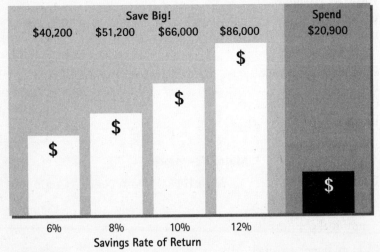

OR SPEND ... Wow! Your habit of weekly lottery tickets will cost you $20,900 if you keep it up for twenty years.

What to Do with the Money You Save: The Magic of Compound Interest

So you've done the hard work. Here's the reward. After you've taken the money you've saved from what you don't need, you can put it to work for you. You use a concept called compound interest that Albert Einstein once called "one of the best inventions in the history of mankind."

Your savings will fund your New Prosperity plan. The point of accumulating money and investing it is not necessarily to build a big stack of money with a finite amount of cash. The key to success is *compounding prosperity*—improving your life and working less. You will have to work less because of the power of compounding, which can work in two ways. First, let's look at the consumption side.

Compounded Consumption

I know this sounds like a wonky phrase from an old economics textbook, but it's savings in reverse. It's spending money on things you may not need—i.e., tobacco products, drugs, cable/satellite television, cell phones, expensive vacations. While I'm not about to make a judgment about what's good or bad, moderate or excessive in your life, you probably already have a good idea about which things you overspend money on. So I'm not going to run down the list of the seven deadly sins. Pick a few spending habits that are costly and that you could do without right about now. Maybe it'll improve your life or attitude if you dump them.

Habits cost money, and the expenditure of that money prevents you from saving it. Say you came to the conclusion that you could live without cable television. If you spend that money over time, no matter how much you enjoy the 100-plus channels available to you (you can watch only one at a time anyway), it goes into somebody else's pot. If you have a hard time saving money—that is, putting money aside for short-, middle-, and long-term investments—you can start with what you're spending now on things that are truly optional. Remember, prosperity has a small price now that yields big dividends later.

Okay, let's assume you've done your little lifestyle audit. The money you saved by not spending it on cable TV, cigarettes, an overpriced vehicle, or whatever goes into an investment fund. Over time, it builds through the miracle of compound interest and you have tens of thousands you didn't think you'd have. Just by auditing your lifestyle and investing that money, you don't have to go out and get another job to earn the extra money for retirement. Your health improves because the time you took indulging in this activity could be spent exercising, which adds years to your life and reduces your total medical bills. You also have more money to enjoy when you attain your New Prosperity. In other words, life gets easier. So let's review a few principles before we move on:

- **Compound interest works because the more you invest, the better it compounds.** Albert Einstein was right, it was a great invention that works for everyone.

- **Compounding works based on the "Rule of 72."** This is the time it takes for a given quantity to double given the rate of growth. It's 72 divided by the rate of return. So at 4% rate of return (what banks were paying on savings accounts in recent years), it will take 18 years for $1,000 to become $2,000 (assuming simple interest). Move up to 6% and the doubling period moves to 12 years; 8% = 9 years; 10% = 7.2 years; 12% = 6 years; 14% = 5 years. If you take no other mathematical principle from this book, remember this one.

- **The investment vehicle in which you are most likely to double your money in the shortest period of time is common stocks.** The average return for the largest 500 stocks over the last 66 years has been just over 10%. If you have 14 years in which to invest, you could conceivably quadruple your money. That means $50,000 at age 51 would grow into $200,000 at age 65 just earning average stock-market returns.

- **Your compounding multiplies by doing nothing.** If you reinvest your dividends and gains and contribute to your investments, your returns will grow even more.

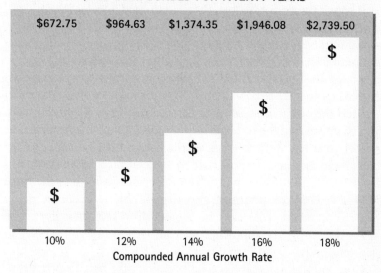

$100 COMPOUNDED FOR TWENTY YEARS

| $672.75 | $964.63 | $1,374.35 | $1,946.08 | $2,739.50 |

Compounded Annual Growth Rate: 10% | 12% | 14% | 16% | 18%

Compounding: A Sports Metaphor

This will be the only intentional sports metaphor I'll use in connection with money. As such, it's a real home run. When I was a boy, I started out playing Wiffle ball in the street with thin plastic bats. The balls were harmless because they had holes in them like Swiss cheese and could never break a window. As my and my playmates' skills improved, we advanced to a Whiffle ball with no holes in it and bigger bats. The ball went further and became a little more threatening to the local fenestration. As we got even bigger and more coordinated, we were able to hit tennis balls with wooden bats. That resulted in a happy exile to the local ballyard next to the Zion Lutheran church, where there was a backstop and no nearby windows except for Pastor Van's house, which was next door to the ball field. Progressing to a sixteen-inch softball, we were still okay at the small ball field, although we continued to get stronger and hit the ball further. Then Little League demanded that we learn the more elusive skill of hitting a hardball. That pushed us into the park with the big boys.

It wasn't the size of the ball that determined how far it would go. There was a delicate interplay between force and mass. A proper swing results in pivoted hips and power coming from your shoulders and back legs compressing the tightly wound mass of the core of a baseball. Then potential energy is transformed into kinetic energy when the bat strikes the ball. It's a beautiful experience when you feel the ball coming off your bat and you know it will travel far. You've transferred the strength of your entire body into a sphere the size of your fist. Yet the crack of the bat and the parabola of the ball's flight are the only post-batting aspects you'll ever enjoy—unless it's a home run that wins a game for your team. It is the force of your energy compounded into a small object. There are many big, strong people who can't hit a baseball to save their lives. The key is the swing, the suppleness of your wrists, and your ability to put your body weight into the arc of the bat.

Compound interest is like a ball coming off a bat. The transmutation of potential to kinetic energy will carry it far depending on your grace and skill. The only skill you'll need in investments is picking out mutual funds or stocks that will compound over time. Then start swinging away.

Summary: What Do You Need?

Have I given you another perspective of the "American way of life" yet? The purpose of this exercise wasn't to make you feel guilty about what you do or don't have, but to help you make some decisions as to what you do or don't need. Let's take a quick look at the highlights:

1. **Do an "amenities audit."** What you don't need can save you money. Total it up. Keep in mind that nearly every one of the appliances in the table on pages 78–79 are direct-selling vehicles that deliver advertising, inane information, and violence into your home. I'm certainly not against the pleasures of a good television, stereo, or computer system (I'm using one to write

this book). Nor is the Internet or cable/satellite television a harbinger of evil. The real question is, Are all of these devices and the information they inundate you with keeping you from what you need to achieve your New Prosperity? Do they provide you comfort, define your personal ecology, or even take out the garbage for you?

2. **Decide what's important.** It may not cost anything. From there, you can do some real New Prosperity planning.

3. **Take your time.** Do the self-surveys. It's a lot to digest. These questions won't go away no matter how much you invest in your 401(k) or mutual funds.

More to the point, economist John Kenneth Galbraith, in his landmark *The Affluent Society,* challenges us directly [italics mine]: "Money must become the *instrument* of the search for self-knowledge. Money must become a tool in the only enterprise worth undertaking for any modern man or woman seriously wishing to find the meaning of their lives: we must use money in order to study ourselves as we are and as we can become.[14]

There's that synergy again between money, meaning, and becoming. It's like a stray cat that keeps returning because you keep putting a saucer of milk out by the back door. Now it's time to take that walk again. Wherever you choose to take your reflective walk, begin today. The future begins with one thought.

CHAPTER 4

Investing in Yourself

How to Invest in Yourself if Your Employment Situation Isn't Contributing to Your Prosperity

"If at first you don't succeed, try something you want to do."

The first thing one notices about Suze Orman is her energy. It seems to flow from every limb the way light emanates from a Christmas tree. She has converted this energy into selling financial products such as annuities and insurance, investing and financial planning. She's been all over the country to promote her books and ideas. She's set records selling her books on cable television. A lot of her best advice she gives away gladly, for she believes that this kind of charity is a circular kind of energy that comes back to her as a psychic reward. Success, however, was something that didn't come early for her, nor did it come easy. Like many late starters, she came to her station in life after a number of setbacks, although she managed to learn and prosper from her failures.

With $300 in her pocket, an old Ford Econoline van, and a degree in social work, Suze Orman headed off to California in the

1970s to find the life that eluded her in Chicago. She ended up in Berkeley, the home of radical chic, where anything could happen. She lived in a bus for a while and chopped down trees for $3.50 an hour until she landed a job as a waitress.

For effervescent souls like Suze, California always seems to be the right kind of place. To make ends meet, she waitressed in the Buttercup Bakery and Restaurant seven days a week. Having the restaurant business in her blood—her father owned Morry's Deli in Chicago—she knew that she could own and run a restaurant of her own. Like many entrepreneurs, she had everything she needed except the money to launch her dream. Her customers appreciated her energy and hard work. They also trusted her when she talked about her dream. After six years, her patrons trusted her enough to raise $50,000 for her restaurant. By 1979, confident she had enough money to start planning, she placed the funds in a Merrill Lynch money market account, then earning 14% during the high-inflation days of the Carter Administration.

A broker, however, thought that Suze could do much better with her money and talked her into signing a margin account, where you can leverage investments through credit and take on the riskiest possible investment strategies. At first she was earning a "quick $100 a week, then $5,000 to $10,000 per month through stock options on oil stocks (then high flyers)." She even wore a pager so that her broker could beep her any time. After three months, however, the market turned the other way and she lost all the original $50,000 when the market for natural resources prices crashed in 1980.

Suze knew she'd never make the money back as a waitress or even as a social worker and was desperate to pay back her investors. "I was scared to death, I didn't know how I'd get out of debt. I ate at Taco Bell." But she did what most horseback riders are told to do time and time again after falling off: she got back on the horse. She also applied for a broker's job at Merrill Lynch. At the time, it was one of the few jobs that required little professional experience (aside from brokerage licenses). More important, it promised huge rewards if you were successful. Since she needed to make a lot of money, Suze thought this the most expedient route.

In 1980, when Suze joined the brokerage industry, it was still a man's game. Brokers would bring in strippers for other brokers' birthdays. Sexually explicit jokes were the norm. When Suze was hired to fill a quota (for female employees), she was immediately handed the book *How to Dress for Success* and had to put $2,000 she didn't have on a credit card for clothing at Macy's. Although the atmosphere repulsed her at times, the 8% to 10% commissions she earned on her financial product sales brought her closer to repaying her debts. As part of the job, she was required to take and pass a NASD Series 7 brokerage exam, which would license her to sell securities. The Series 7 exam is known as a tough exam, but you can't sell securities without passing it. The first time she took it, she failed it.

"My heart broke. I *wanted* this. I liked what I was learning. So I took the exam one week later and passed it. In addition, I wanted to make Mom and Dad proud. They never had much money. My dad studied to be a lawyer, but needed $900 to study for the bar. He ended up using that money for a chicken restaurant that later burned down."

At her new job, not only did Suze learn the tricks of the trade, she did something almost no one did at the time: She sued Merrill Lynch while she was working there. She wanted her money back. A professional broker now, she realized that her original $50,000 had been placed in "unsuitable" investments for her investment background. The investments her broker recommended were not in line with the amount of risk she was willing to take at the time, especially considering that it wasn't even her money that was placed in high-risk vehicles. Besides, as a broker, she discovered there were laws that protected investors like her. Moreover, after reading Merrill Lynch literature on matching clients with appropriate investments, she felt taken. She had a strong case, so the brokerage house returned her money.

Around the same time, Suze was doing a land-office business selling millions of dollars worth of single-premium annuities, a popular tax shelter before Congress slammed the door on it several years later. One of the products she sold was underwritten by a company called Baldwin-United, which later filed for bankruptcy. She was told by her bosses that they "wouldn't sell it if it wasn't okay." By 1983, she had left Merrill Lynch to work at Prudential-Bache. After several major changes in the tax code, she was selling single-premium, whole-life insurance plans, which was another hot tax shelter at the time. Despite her rough experience with the business, she had mastered the art of selling tax shelters, becoming one of the top salespersons in the country for that product. In addition, she was the only woman vice president for Prudential-Bache in her office at the time.

It still bothered Suze, though, that people like herself could be fleeced so easily, so she started her own firm in 1987 to focus on investment advice to help people avoid the risks that she had encountered the hard way. It was still too easy to lose your nest egg in vehicles that financial services firms marketed aggressively by promising high returns and disguising risk. Some of the literature provided investors to explain risk was so densely worded that you needed a lawyer and an accountant to figure out how much risk you were taking. Suze was determined not to see any more families ruined by bad investments.

Suze's desire to help others with their investments was spurred by the misfortune that seemed to run in her family when it came to investments and business. Suze's grandfather, who came over from Kiev, used to run a live-chicken store. They used to kill and pluck the chickens for customers; her grandmother would make chicken liver. The store did well, so her grandfather bought a boarding-house with her father. One day a woman fell off a banister and injured herself so badly she became a quadriplegic. The resulting lawsuit financially ruined her grandparents. Suze's father, who followed his father into the food business, was burned badly in a fire that destroyed his chicken restaurant. The resulting damage to his lungs left him seriously ill for the rest of his life, making every breath a struggle. So he had to start over at 60. In spite of his own hardships, she recalls that he would cry when somebody won on *Wheel of Fortune.* Her father felt good that *others* were winning money. He cried at the prospect of prosperity, something that Suze regarded as his sense of generosity.

As a result of her own and her family's experience, Suze has developed a philosophy of money that includes generosity as one of the cornerstones. Investing is a simple process, she notes, but there's a certain energy connected with having money, respecting it, and giving it away.

"Rip up a dollar bill and see the horror in people's faces," she offers with amusement. "Money has an energy all of its own. Money is alive. Don't squeeze it so hard it hurts. Those in serious debt should give money to a place of worship or nonprofit. Then stay open to receive all that's coming your way. Money gets attracted to you. I was depressed one day and sent a check to PBS. I was totally happy. Then I noticed whenever I sent out checks, more money came in."

Suze is not encouraging people to spend beyond their means, but is referring to the transformative power of money. It isn't solely a medium of exchange. It represents the labor and the spirit behind the labor needed to earn it. Money is like a telephone wire. Both carry energy and convey information a long way. Like experience, money has the power to enhance, change, or even destroy our lives. When we exchange our experience, knowledge, and labor for money, we are passing along our energy to others. Suze's idea of money as a circular energy that returns to us in another form also applies to how we regard our work lives. When examining how we define prosperity, we need to look at the energy of our labors. Our work is more than a work-for-money exchange, it's a symbol of what we're willing to do for prosperity. So the question here is, Is our labor worth what we receive in return? Does the energy add or detract from our lives?

What Investing in Yourself Really Means

Blindly putting money into a stock, mutual fund, or bond without knowing what you want from it is like getting the wrong kind of battery for a portable device. Only one battery will have the right voltage, fit the battery slot, and do the job correctly. Few people realize that they need to invest in themselves as well. The phrase "recharge your batteries" has great currency in our culture, but few heed it. Investing, like building a home or getting a paycheck, is a transfer of energy.

We live in a world strangely disconnected from the past. We seem to forget all the energy we've wasted on dead-end jobs, junk cars, bad relationships, and lousy investments. Sometimes the world overwhelms us. We are bombarded with information all the time. So it's hard to walk away and recharge our batteries. It's hard to escape the information coming at us from all angles. So let's sort through the basics and do an "energy audit" of the information we really need to know. Let's look at the key principles to create a New Prosperity:

New Prosperity Principles

1. You can't spend more than you make. Reduce your expenses and invest the savings. Decide what you want to do with the money and your time. In other words, you really can't expend more life/labor energy than you have, no matter what is said in the advertising that assaults you from every angle.

2. Show me the money. Where is your money coming from and where can it go? Know the source and amount of your life/labor energy. Exactly how much does your household take home after taxes? Do you have other sources of income?

3. Put money in growth-oriented investments now through a company plan or one you set up. Use mutual funds, stocks, and other income vehicles to anchor your plan. This is not only a type of storage vehicle for your life/labor energy, it generates wealth over time. If you're not taking advantage of every tax-deferred vehicle you can, you're wasting your energy.

4. Live the life you want by investing in yourself. This redirects your life energy back into your life. This principle involves the most dedication to your definition of prosperity. It's also the most fun because you'll be learning, embracing new ideas, and changing your life. No matter how old you are now, it's never too late to invest in yourself.

While I was doing research for *The Investment Club Book,* I encountered women in their sixties, seventies, and eighties who were not only learning how to use computers for the first time, but running businesses with them. They were also sharing their newfound wisdom with their children, grandchildren, and great-grandchildren. The new technology brought them a new prosperity. In learning how to analyze and invest in growth stocks on their own, they were simply redirecting their life energies back into their minds and investment portfolios and making money at the same time.

By creating your New Prosperity plan, you are building your own utopia. Oscar Wilde once said that "a map of the world that does not include Utopia is not worth glancing at." How do you find that utopia when the bills keep coming in, you feel like you'll be working until you're 80, and midlife has hit you hard?

Living by the New Prosperity principles is a start. Another way is to eliminate the noise and static in your life. You may need to redirect your resources. There's a reason for the success of books on simplification over the past several years. The simplification bible *Your Money or Your Life* by Joe Dominguez and Vicki Robin has consistently been a bestseller in the face of a booming stock market that could lead people to live high on the hog. A former stockbroker, Dominguez decided to live on a modest income and taught others to appreciate the "life value" of time and money. When he died of cancer a young man in January 1997, he told his loved ones that he left with "a clean bill of *death*." He had done what he needed to do and left behind a legacy of knowledge and hope rather than a residue of regret. He founded the New Road Map Foundation in Seattle to teach people how to find their utopia with less money and more satisfaction.

The path to utopia by way of the New Prosperity is astoundingly simple. You have to decide to reorient yourself toward investment—in growth, yourself, and your own time. You have to dispense with conventional wisdom on a number of scores: perhaps consider a new job or "downshift" to a quieter, less hectic way of life. This may seem like a handful, but it's all still possible and necessary if you want to bring New Prosperity into your life. These decisions will involve a downscaling of what you consume. While it may be easy to identify problem areas, it's harder to identify what to scale back.

Questioning Your Livelihood

Assuming you've done the requisite auditing of your lifestyle to determine what you can redirect into your New Prosperity investment plan, the much more difficult question involves what you can do with your livelihood. If you are satisfied with your work and earnings, move on to the next section. If some balance is missing in your work life, let's take another walk in the woods.

The nature of work itself is changing, so there's no reason to believe that you should work for twenty or more years at the same place doing the same thing for small annual increases in your salary. Here's information about how the workplace has changed and how you might come up with a new work plan to attain the New Prosperity:

- Some 2.7 million to 6 million workers are in "contingent" employment—that is, they work jobs of limited duration on contract. If you have a specialty, this may suit you better than a job you work at every day.[1]

- Independent contractors comprise nearly 7% of the workforce, or 8.3 million workers.[2] In an era of downsizing and rightsizing you may have a better chance working for a company as a contractor. Of course, these jobs don't always pay full benefits, so you have to find a firm that hires out contractors that will cover your health care or will pay enough for you to cover those costs yourself.

- There's a widespread myth that workers are staying with the same employer for several decades. Only 29% of workers aged 55 to 64 worked for the same employer for twenty years or more. The median (half above, half below) employment tenure for a person in the same position is about four years. So workers are staying in one place less often and moving on a lot. The "thirty-years-and-out" single-job scenario is virtually nonexistent.[3]

More workers are moving from job to job because a vibrant economy presents better opportunities. That means more flexibility in the form of contract work, flexible hours, off-site work, or telecommuting to work in locales that offer a better quality of life. The new positions are not where you think they are. It's commonly accepted that Rust Belt industries are on the wane in most Western countries and high-tech industries have replaced them as the engines of our economy's growth. In a general sense, that's true. Looking at where the actual growth in jobs is, however, tells a different story. The new jobs are in rather mundane-sounding service-support industries. While these may not seem glamorous, they cater to a population that is getting older, is more interested in personal services and health care, and is willing to pay for them.

THE 25 FASTEST-GROWING OCCUPATIONS, 1994–2005 (AS PROJECTED BY THE BUREAU OF LABOR STATISTICS)

Occupation (Only occupations with at least 100,000 employees in 1994 are included)	Employment		Net job growth (thous.)	Percent change in employment
	1984	2005		
Personal and home care aides	179	391	212	118%
Home health aides	420	848	428	102%
Systems analysts	483	928	445	92%
Computer engineers	195	372	177	91%
All other computer scientists	149	283	134	90%
Physical therapists	102	183	81	79%
Residential counselors	165	290	125	76%
Human services workers	168	293	125	74%
Medical assistants	206	327	121	59%
Paralegals	110	175	65	59%
Teachers, special education	388	593	205	53%

Occupation (Only occupations with at least 100,000 employees in 1994 are included)	Employment		Net job growth (thous.)	Percent change in employment
	1984	2005		
Amusement and recreation attendants	267	406	139	52%
Corrections officers	310	468	158	51%
Guards	867	1,282	415	48%
All other health service workers	157	224	67	43%
Dental hygienists	127	180	53	42%
Dental assistants	190	269	79	42%
Adjustment clerks	373	521	148	40%
Sales workers in securities and financial services	246	335	89	36%
Bill and account collectors	250	342	92	37%
Emergency medical technicians	138	187	49	36%
Management analysts	231	312	81	35%
Bakers, bread and pastry	170	230	60	35%
Instructors and coaches, sports and physical training	283	381	98	35%
Food service and lodging managers	579	771	192	33%
All 25 occupations	6,753	10,591	3,838	57%

SOURCE: Bureau of Labor Statistics

ABOVE-AVERAGE JOB GROWTH (BY INDUSTRY)

Industry	1992–2005 Employment Change (percent)
Health services	43.4
Educational services	28.4
Food service	33
Social services	93.1
Personnel supply services	56.6
Computer services	95.7
Hotels/lodging	40.5
Amusement/recreation	39.1
Management/public relations	69.5
Child-care services	73
Agricultural services	40.5
Motion picture production	60.8

SOURCE: U.S. Department of Labor/Bureau of Labor Statistics' 1994–95 *Career Guide to Industries*

BELOW-AVERAGE JOB GROWTH (BY INDUSTRY)

Industry	1992–2005 Employment Change (percent)
Apparel manufacturing	−24.4
Telephone communications	−20.6
Electronics manufacturing	−16.3
Textile manufacturing	−15
Oil and gas extraction	−14.3

Industry	1992–2005 Employment Change (percent)
Steel manufacturing	−10.5
Mining	−6.8
Motor vehicle manufacturing	−6.1
Federal government	−5.2
Chemicals (except drugs)	−4.0
Food processing	−0.4
Aerospace manufacturing	2.5

SOURCE: U.S. Department of Labor/Bureau of Labor Statistics

In the tables on pages 94–97, you have a clear view of the expanding and contracting of the labor markets. For many, the big surprises in the below-average growth industries are federal government jobs, telephone communications positions, and aerospace jobs. In a global economy, nearly every manufacturing operation can be moved to an area of cheap labor and nearby resources. China, Mexico, Indonesia, India, and South America are greeting multinational corporations with open arms. If you are employed in these below-average growth industries, you need to look ahead. Unless you get retrained in a high-growth industry, you could be vulnerable at the wrong time in your life.

The growth is basically in the human services, except for the more technical professions, which require a higher level of education and training. According to the *Workforce 2020* report published by the Hudson Institute, the occupations that are expected to grow more than 50% until the year 2005 are:

Personal, home-health, and home-care aides (up 102% to 118%)

Computer systems analysts, engineers, and scientists (up 90% to 92%)

Physical therapists, residential counselors, human service workers, and medical assistants (up 59% to 79%)

Paralegals (up 59%)

Amusement/recreation attendants (up 52%)

Corrections officers and guards (up 51%)[4]

While it's a little distressing to see the growth in prison employees—and inmates—the human service-industry growth is encouraging. Human-service workers can be self-employed, work on contract, gain flexible work schedules, and adapt to a number of changing situations. You can work directly for a doctor, hospital, or home-health-care company or be your own boss. You can often also choose to work as many or as few hours as you like. Even better news, as noted by the Hudson Institute study, is that "the jobs that are growing most rapidly in numbers also pay the best. These jobs require increasingly high levels of skill and knowledge."

Establishing your New Prosperity plan via the employment market requires a high degree of vigilance, however. The global economy will demand the best-trained workers at every level at the lowest possible cost. Capital always flows where labor and resources are not necessarily at a premium. If your company or industry is on the endangered list, you need to do some serious research about a new or improved occupation. Not even high-technology workers are immune from obsolescence. In the post-cold-war global economy, jobs will move from developed countries to less developed countries.

In researching *The Judas Economy* William Wolman and Anne Colamosca found that those who believe that the American economy will continue to be an unfettered job machine are deluding themselves and should prepare themselves for "the great post-cold-war divorce" from the conventional thinking that job and income growth will benefit any educated worker.

So as capital has emerged as an equal opportunity employer throughout the post-cold-war world, the tendency of wages to become equal at all points on the globe will work with great force. For workers in the emerging world, the prospects are the ascent of their relative wages toward a new heaven. For workers in the developed world, the prospects are for a descent in their relative wages toward a new hell.[5]

As you age, however, the news isn't all dire. Your experience and your ability to learn new skills work in your favor. According to James Challenger, president of the outplacement firm Challenger, Gray & Christmas, "over the next ten years as the average age of the American worker increases, older workers will possess two of the characteristics most prized by employers: they will be experienced and they will be affordable."[6] A key strategy in attaining your New Prosperity is buying flexibility by investing in yourself. That's the best way of avoiding the slings and arrows of the global economy.

Education and Your New Prosperity

The formula for advancement has always been rather simple: Get educated and work hard for someone else or start your own business. After looking at your checkbook, you may have discovered a long time ago that despite your—and your significant other's—hard work, you're not keeping up with the cost of living. Despite a supposedly robust, job-producing economy and a bull stock market, real median incomes at the end of 1996 were still about $2,000 below what they were in 1988, if adjusted for inflation. One factor that separates families moving forward from those falling behind is the amount of education one has.

Education plays an important role in increasing wages and standards of living. Research by Nobel Prize–winning economist Gary Becker has shown that those with more education consistently outearn their less educated peers. In inflation-adjusted (1994) dollars, high school graduates earned about $10,000 per year more than those who were not high school graduates. Moving up the educational ladder leads to even more dramatic earnings gains. A person with a bachelor's degree earned twice as much as the high school graduate—that's $20,000 more. The worker with the advanced degree earned about $20,000 per year more than the person with the bachelor's degree (around $60,000 annually). This is hardly new information, but worth remembering when you think about ways of making more money in the workplace.

MEDIAN ANNUAL SALARIES BY EDUCATIONAL LEVEL

Bachelor's degree	$34,736
Master's degree	$45,292

SOURCE: U.S. Department of Labor/BLS, 1996

While an advanced degree is no guarantee of higher wages, getting the right kind of education or training in the right industry or profession can give you an edge that will improve your income and flexibility now and in the future. That means you'll have more money to save and invest and you can fully fund your New Prosperity investment plan. Should you enroll in a Ph.D. or MBA program tomorrow? This may not be the right thing to do for you or your industry. It's more important to choose an industry/occupation/profession that provides you with the most flexibility. You should of course enjoy what you're doing. It'll make the transition a lot smoother and give you a smile at both ends of the day.

So who has time to go back to college? If you are like most of us, you just can't drop everything and enroll in a doctorate program, lose that full-time income, and hang around a college for the next five years or so. Fortunately, there are a number of more reasonable options.

Certificate Programs. These part-time (usually at night or on weekends) programs are short in duration and boost your knowledge/skill base for a fraction of what it would cost to get a full-time degree. Some 500 reputable universities and community colleges offer them. They cover everything from architectural technology to zoo management. They'll also be less stressful than full degree programs, since you probably won't be graded. Just show up and do the work.

Adult or Continuing Education. These courses are often taught at local high schools or colleges and provide low-stress environments in which to enhance your computer, money-management, clerical, managerial, and other service-oriented skills. Check your local library to see what's offered in your area.

Community Colleges. This is America's best-kept education secret. Nearly every county in an urban area has a community college offering a wide array of programs; the focus is often on basic academic skills (English, composition, math, or business communications) or on crafts and trades such as construction, landscaping, nursing, or food service.

Graduate Degrees. Many are now offered at night or on weekends, although you can expect to spend from $12,000 to $35,000 for a two-year program (either a master's or an MBA). They can be well worth your money and time if the knowledge makes you a more capable manager. Companies of all types still pay premiums for qualified, experienced, and savvy managers.

Community Education. If you just open up your local paper, you'll be amazed at the number and variety of low-cost classes taught at libraries, community centers, senior centers, churches, temples, town halls, high schools, fraternal organizations, and park districts. You can brush up on anything from language skills to basic investing. None of these classes costs very much; quite a few are free. Just be careful to avoid financial-broker types who are offering "educational seminars" designed to rope you in as a client.

There's little you *can't* do if you educate yourself to do it. It's the one enhancement you can make in your employment that is irrevocable and you can start any time. You can also start a business, but that will take considerably more research and skill. Education is the best route to learning about a new business. Try a number of the educational options I've listed to see what may be right for you. There are hundreds of books on starting a new business. When you

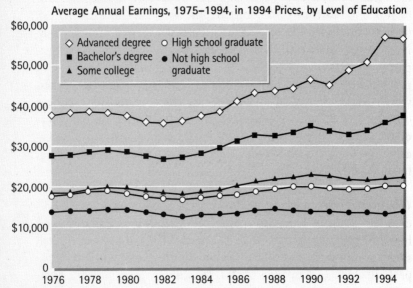

ON AVERAGE, BETTER-EDUCATED WORKERS EARN BETTER
Average Annual Earnings, 1975–1994, in 1994 Prices, by Level of Education

◇ Advanced degree   ○ High school graduate
■ Bachelor's degree   ● Not high school
▲ Some college   graduate

N.B. Data were adjusted for inflation using the Consumer Price Index corrected by diminishing the reported rate of price increase by 1.1 percentage points annually.

SOURCE: Census Bureau and Bureau of Labor Statistics

stop learning, you stop living. Keep on learning and growing. It's a bulwark of prosperity.

Taking Time Off and Giving to Others

So far we've laid out the bad news on employment and the economy and had you busy reeducating yourself. Now it's time to take a break. The average American has more free time than at any other point during the past three decades, reports researchers John Robinson and Geoffrey Godbey in *Time for Life*. Unfortunately, the largest single chunk of leisure time—some fifteen hours per day—is spent in front of the television, according to the group TV-Free America. That's more than double the time we spend socializing and nearly twelve times more time than we spend reading, with hobbies, or educating ourselves.[7]

You may be unconsciously addicted to television to the point that it's your drug of choice. The truth is, you'll never achieve your New Prosperity with this addiction keeping you down. New Prosperity means working less and having more time for active engagement in the things you want to do with the people you want to be with—on your own terms. Television is almost exclusively passive.

What would you do if you had more time? A surprising number of people can't answer that. For the prosperity-challenged, here are a few suggestions elicited from 100-year-olds, who were asked what factors contributed to their long lives[8]:

Getting Plenty of Sleep and Eating Good Food. It requires time to do both. With the assault of the perpetual workplace (working at home, telecommuting) and fast food, people don't take the time to sleep enough and eat well. Having regular sleep patterns and eating properly can add years to your life.

Exercising. This is a perennial that all too many people say they have no time for. A healthy body needs regular exercise.

Education. Keeping your mind fresh and invigorated involves infusing your brain with knowledge.

Helping Others. Local, regional, and national charities would rather have your time than your dollars. You'll feel better about your community and others. It's better to give than to receive.

Helping Your Family. Do you have a will or living trust? You need one to ensure that your loved ones are provided for when you are gone. Better yet, help them out in this life. Spend some time with them. Remember your personal ecology from chapter 2? It involves relationships that are nurturing. You can't have such relationships without spending time on them. Our relationships with family members reflect our relationship with the world. Caring can go a long way.

Exercising Your Spirit. We all need it. It doesn't matter if you practice an established religion or hike down the Grand Canyon, if spirit is missing from your life, your life is not whole and prosperity will elude you. You choose the best way of celebrating the spirit.

Working Closer to Home. Fortune magazine found that an average of 57 hours a week were spent by 2,000 of its readers working *and* commuting. As one who is writing this book while spending some 25,000 miles a year commuting, I can tell you there is a better way. You can make your commute more productive or you can start a home-based business. There's always contract work or the contingent employment that I mentioned earlier. Some people like to have a long distance between work and home. If so, make that distance a time of reflection, organization, or relaxation.

Investing in yourself is about making choices. You don't need to blindly plunk money into a stock or mutual fund. Money should work for you in the way you want it to serve your idea of prosperity. All of the suggestions in this book are merely that. You need to chart your own course.

CHAPTER 5

Getting Smart, Getting Savvy Fast: Quick and Direct Ways of Saving Money for Your New Prosperity Plan

Easy Ways to Cut Spending and Start Saving

"If you can't live long, live often."

Life forces particular mythologies on us. You can't spend as much as you want. You have to spend it all because you can't take it with you. Leave something for your children. Leave *nothing* for your children, they won't appreciate what you had to do to get the money. Get an education. Degrees mean nothing if they're going to lay you off when you hit 50 and make too much money. Get married to someone with means. Money causes problems in a marriage. Work hard to get ahead. All the work in the world won't buy you time. These are troubling dichotomies. How do we get to the point where we can define our New Prosperity? As much as we'd like to lead a simpler life, there's always something preventing us from getting there. Whether it's a mortgage, that extra degree, the kid's education, or the costs of living, there are obstacles aplenty.

Before we examine the obstacles—and bring them down like the Berlin Wall—I want you to meet someone who had the right idea in mind when it came to pursuing her own vision of New Prosperity.

Married at 20, with a B.A. in economics and a master's degree in education, Priscilla Salvi-Itscoitz landed a plum job with the Commerce Department as a junior business economist. The job paid well and was civil service. The only problem was, as a self-proclaimed "people person," Priscilla hated the position, which involved crunching numbers that ultimately disappeared into obscure government documents. After a year and a half, she quit.

She then became a working mother, raising two daughters while helping her husband through medical school. After he completed his education, her husband paid all the bills in the marriage; she only signed the tax returns. When the girls got ready to go out on their own, however, she suddenly had to look at things differently: Her marriage of twenty-three years was coming to an end. She and her husband, who was now a highly trained specialist, decided to separate. Despite the fact that she had worked to put her husband through medical school, had been there during the hard times, and had basically raised the girls alone, she ended up with only a small settlement. On her own now, she had to support herself.

Taking a tax-preparation course at H&R Block, she developed an interest in financial services, which she felt she knew nothing about. Working as a volunteer and taking a few courses at a local community college combined with several odd jobs provided a crash course in life skills. She had a long way to go. She was promised a position at a subsidiary of Travelers Insurance doing retirement planning for employees of a large hospital, so she studied for and obtained her Series 6 National Association of Securities Dealers license and her health and life insurance license. Unfortunately, the promised position fell through.

"I knew things had changed when the first section I picked up [at the beginning of my financial education] was the *Washington Post* business section," Priscilla recalls of her late-start education. Ironically, it was then she discovered "how little people plan for retirement."

So she looked for work again in a bad job market. Priscilla's education and age made her overqualified for most entry-level financial services positions. So she took a job as a teller in a credit union, not disclosing that she had two degrees. She kept telling herself that a better job awaited her, one that combined financial services with human services. In other words, she wanted to provide a service, but not to sell it. She became a part-time worker with the United Seniors Health Cooperative (USHC), a nonprofit Washington, D.C.–based service that is one of the leading services providing counseling on Medicare and related health-insurance issues. In November 1994, she started the 24-hour-a-week position, but actually ended up working closer to 60 hours. Although there were no benefits or holidays, she found an enjoyable niche counseling the elderly and advocating for them on the thorny rules regarding federal health insurance programs and long-term care insurance. Her work was recognized and she was promoted to a 30-hour position with 3/4 benefits, all the while she worked the hours of a full-time job and a half.

Two years later, she was finally offered a full-time position with full benefits and a 403(b) defined-contribution plan that offered her another tax-deferred vehicle to save for her retirement. It was a real leap forward because her employer contributed 10%. "I put 10% [of my annual] salary into the 403(b) because I wanted to contribute as much as possible. I was starting late. It was eleven years since the [marital] separation and I was working my butt off to get this job. I came out of a deep, dark pit. How was I ever going to do this? I took seminars and courses. My employer took a chance on me. They liked my personal qualities and my diverse education and interests."

Despite virtually creating and then landing the position she wanted, Priscilla now had to learn how to invest *her* retirement funds. Her insurance job provided some background, but it was scarcely enough, so she hired a fee-only financial planner, took an American Association for Retired Persons course for midlife women, and put a portion of her ex-husband's pension into a nondeductible individual retirement account (IRA). She put 80% of these funds into growth stocks and placed the remainder in zero-coupon U.S. Treasury bonds. A separate portfolio of government securities, utility stocks, and a few high-dividend stocks made up the rest of her investment plan, aside from her retirement funds. The money for her portfolio came from her portion of the proceeds of the sale of the family home.

"After one-third of a century of not having a career outside the home, there was no way I was going to catch up in terms of earning power," Priscilla remembers during her initial financial planning phase. "It was twenty-nine years from the date of the marriage to when the divorce became final. I was offered jobs selling insurance, but that is not me. I'm passionate about educating people about making important choices because *I've* done it. I've lived it."

Her lifestyle now is comfortable, in her opinion, although she hardly lives lavishly. She still drives a 1978 Buick LeSabre with 220,000 miles on it and takes the subway to work in Washington. She bought a small condo and likes the fact she can walk to the Metro and a number of shops in her neighborhood. "I could've been retired with a pension by now [had she stayed in her government job all this time]; it's stark how behind I was. There's no way I would've had the guts to put 80% of my IRA money into stocks without educating myself on financial matters."

As the manager of USHC's health insurance counseling program, Salvi-Itscoitz developed one of the finest programs of its type in the country. I've referred to her program a number of times when I need a no-nonsense guide on long-term care or Medicare. Although she started over at a time when most are thinking about a place in the sun, she's still working on her "five-year financial plan." She wants her portfolio to earn $20,000 a year for her, but as of this writing, it wasn't quite there, despite some excellent years in the stock market. Although she's not quite there yet, she's well on her way to a New Prosperity. Now she has an even better job with the American Association of Retired Persons, applying her knowledge for the largest national organization of its kind.

Savviness and the New Prosperity

Priscilla Salvi-Itscoitz acquired the savvy she needed the hard way. Like Priscilla, you should know that before you can even consider investing, you need a certain savviness about the basic financial facts of life. You can't invest unless you are managing your affairs at the checkbook level. One of the most common questions asked any financial adviser is "Where do I find the money to invest?" The answer hinges on expenses you can control and expenses you can reduce. Here are some of the everyday ways of saving money and the obstacles you may need to overcome to employ them.

Managing Your Mortgage

If you are working on trimming your mortgage payment, there are some fundamentals you should know. If you have a conventional thirty- or fifteen-year loan and keep paying the specified monthly payment, you are paying tens of thousands of dollars to the bank that you needn't pay. You can easily pay off your mortgage early, but it will require some discipline and extra payments. Once you do that, you'll have freedom to do much more in your later years with much less because one of the biggest expenditures in your monthly budget will be gone. Here's an example:

For every dollar you borrow in a mortgage, you pay back $2 to $4 in interest. That means a $100,000 mortgage at 9% for thirty years will cost you a total of $289,666.80. Such a deal for the bank! Not only do lenders have you locked in to their payment plan—until you refinance or sell the house—they're making money on the money they lent you and the escrow you probably hold in their account. Escrow is the money you put into a separate, typically non-interest-bearing account to pay for taxes and insurance on your home. This is the bank's little insurance fund that assures that money is put aside for these items. You should be making money on these funds, but most people don't even realize that they're not. If a bank is using your money, make them pay interest. Banks are charging you interest on the use of their money! Moreover, under their "Rule of 72," the interest payments are skewed to be higher in the earlier years, because most people sell their homes in the first seven years. So the banks are legally getting their money up front. The payment works out like this:

$100,000, THIRTY-YEAR MORTGAGE AT 9% ANNUAL PERCENTAGE RATE

Interest	$750.00
Principal	$54.63
Total monthly payment*	$804.63

*excludes taxes, insurance and other fees[1]

Okay, so there's a reason why the banks are making money and don't hand out toasters anymore. What can you do about it? *The key is regular prepayments on principal.* This isn't making an extra mortgage payment per month, it's making extra payments directly to principal. Any bank will allow you to do this; most don't advertise or encourage it. Some even charge you money to do it if you choose one of their "mortgage accelerator" ripoffs. This is your own mortgage freedom program. For each payment to principal, you are also cutting your total interest bill, since interest is based on the total amount of money outstanding on the mortgage. Knock down principal on a steady basis and you save tens of thousands and retire that mortgage note earlier. Here's how this can work:

PAYING DOWN PRINCIPAL ON A $100,000, 30-YEAR MORTGAGE

Additional $50 payment per month × 30	$14,050.00
Total payments to bank	$240,151.03
Savings in dollars	$63,565.77
Savings in loan term (years you don't pay)	6.6 years[2]

These savings are enough for a potential college education or two and more money freed up near or during your retirement. There's also a feeling of accomplishment in paying off your mortgage six and a half years early. The rule here is to pay what you can afford to in terms of an extra principal payment. The more money you slap down on principal, the sooner you can pay it and the interest off.

According to Ed Mrkvicka, a former bank president turned consumer advocate who made the above calculations, no bank will volunteer this information. They want you to stick to their amortization table until you pay off the note because they make more money that way. Although most people are sheepish when it comes to calling the shots with banks, it's as easy as negotiating a new payment plan and writing that extra check.

Getting a New Mortgage

You may be able to save money right away if current mortgage rates are at least one point lower than the rate on your present loan. Refinancing your mortgage is a primary way of reducing that monthly payment through interest rate alone. You need to be careful, however. Banks like to make money on every step of the financing process, but if you are shrewd and firm in your negotiations, you can get the good deal you deserve. Here are a few guidelines:

LATE-STARTER TIP

If you commit to a mortgage prepayment plan, go back to the retirement goals worksheet on pages 46–48 and subtract the mortgage debt you thought you were going to pay, if applicable. Do the numbers look better?

- **Go for the lowest rate and points.** Keep in mind that points are nothing less than pure profit for the bank. If you "finance" the points by adding them to your loan amount, that effectively raises the amount you have to pay back. If you plan to stay in your home for a decade or so, you can opt for higher points and a lower interest rate. When looking for financing, shop around at several banks, including out-of-state institutions. Mortgage financing is an extremely competitive business, so if you settle on one lender, negotiate for your best deal. Current rates are usually posted in the real estate or business sections of local newspapers. Also check *Your Money, Money,* and *Kiplinger's Personal Finance* magazines for the best national deals. On the Internet, the Bank Rate Monitor (http://www.bankrate.com) posts even more current information.

- **All fees and expenses are negotiable.** Banks are fond of milking you for seemingly trivial fees for documentation preparation, handling, and other items that are pure profit. Try to cut as many of those fees out before you get down to the closing. Banks are already making big money on interest and points. If your banker doesn't want to cut the junk fees, take your business elsewhere.

- **Avoid special options that you don't need.** Items that are tacked onto your mortgage payment may include "credit-life" or "disability insurance" policies. These exorbitantly priced plans pay the bank if something happens to you. If you have adequate health, life, and disability insurance, you don't need these horrible plans. Mortgage prepayment plans that charge you for setup and documentation are also money wasters.

- **Adjutable rate mortgages (ARMs) should be avoided unless you know you are moving soon.** An ARM offers great short-term teaser rates that are usually a point or more below thirty-year rates. They are best used for those staying in their home for under two years. ARMs are quick to catch up with rises in interest rates and are like snails when rates come down. Although the initial monthly payment may sound affordable with this plan, keep in mind that you have no control over interest rates. In 1994, a year of practically no inflation, interest rates were increased four times. You want your mortgage to be a fixed cost that you can pay off early. If you have an ARM that can be converted to a fixed-rate loan with low fees (under $200), ask your bank to lock you in at a decent rate.

- **Don't get a fifteen-year loan if you don't have to.** Remember, no matter what the term of your loan is now, you control the term if you pay off principal early. Banks love fifteen-year loans even more than thirty-year loans because they get interest back at double the rate in half the time. Banks count on the fact that most people will move before the term is up and they've gotten even more money up front with a fifteen-year loan. By doubling your principal payment on your thirty-year loan, you can create a fifteen-year loan for the price of a thirty-year note—and save tens of thousands in the process.

- **Don't pay your taxes and insurance through an escrow account.** Unless you are required to create them by law or contract, escrow accounts are a bad financial deal for you. Almost none of them pay interest, so the bank is using your money when it could be earning interest for you. Worried that you'll forget to set aside enough money for taxes? Automatically withdraw the correct amount into a money market fund and have the tax bill sent directly to you. That way you get a biannual reminder and earn some interest. My wife and I have an automatic withdrawal from our checking account into a tax-free money market account, so we don't pay any federal taxes on the interest we earn on our savings. We had to fight our bank to do this, but in the end we got our way and it was worth it.

- **Don't pay private mortgage insurance (PMI) if you don't have to.** Banks require this expensive addition to your monthly mortgage payment if your equity, usually the down payment at purchase, is less than 20% of your home's purchase price. This anti-consumer policy ensures the *lender* in the event of default. It provides no benefit to you whatsoever. If your equity exceeds 20%, your lender should drop PMI, which is added to your principal and interest payment every month. Unless federal law changes, lenders are not required to drop PMI after the 20% mark. If you are buying a new house, try to pony up the 20% down payment to avoid it.

Drowning the Debt Monster

Now that you've looked at lowering payments on arguably the biggest monthly fee you have, it's time to tackle some day-to-day debts. You've probably already seen these numbers several times on the evening news, but let's do a little review.

In 1996, consumers charged some $1 trillion on credit cards, with about $500 billion of that amount "revolving." That means instead of paying off the balance on their cards each month, consumers paid only the nondeductible fees on the balance, according to a Consumer Federation of America (CFA) study from which the following is cited.[3] Moreover:

- Of the 56 to 60 million households that revolve debt—up to 60% of all American households—their annual debts averaged $6,000 and required $1,000 in interest and fees every year, the study revealed.

- The typical family in this profile had disposable income of $20,000 with total credit card debts including finance charges and fees of $10,000.

- More than 1 million Americans applied for personal bankruptcy in 1997.

The CFA, which conducted the aforementioned survey, is usually fairly dead-on when it comes to these unpleasant subjects. To many, credit cards have become the push buttons to our daily dreams, or at least they make buying what we can't afford easier. In reality, though, like so many other elements of our consumption-oriented culture, credit cards are making somebody else rich and keeping us in debt, further distancing us from prosperity.

Despite the steady descent of interest rates since the early 1980s, average credit-card interest rates have hovered near 18%. Most banks are not regulated when it comes to this onerous charge; only a handful of states impose a limit. There's always a temptation to get another card. It's not uncommon for the average household to receive three to five credit solicitations per *week*. And if you're already in debt, you can get into more debt with credit cards quickly. In fact, the more in debt you are, the less likely it is that you will ever get *out* of debt if your income is consistently less than what you owe. You'll simply be paying the interest down on a revolving line of credit that never stops revolving. Welcome to the credit merry-go-round.

Is the Debt Monster Devouring Your Income?

How do you know if the debt monster is eating you alive? Here's a simple evaluation. Also read on for more details on how to curtail and pay down debt.

- You are paying only the minimum payment of each monthly bill.

- Your total nondeductible debt service, which are payments excluding mortgage, exceeds 20% of your monthly take-home pay.

- You are charging items like (nonbusiness) meals, sundries (toothpaste, candy), and other nonessential everyday items.

- You feel you need a loan just to pay off your credit-card bills.

If you answered yes to any of the above questions, you'll need to frame a debt-reduction plan. Even if you are saving for retirement through company plans or IRAs, having stifling debts can prohibit you from investing. Basically, you can pay off the bills one at a time or consolidate them into a home-equity loan. I personally prefer the former rather than the latter. Although home-equity debt is tax deductible, you should keep in mind that it is a second mortgage. If you can't pay this loan off, a lien is placed on your home and you could lose it.

Debt-Reduction Weapons

Whichever route you choose, here are some swords to slay the debt monster. Choose as many options as possible to rid yourself of debt:

- **You need only one credit card if you can use it wisely.** You're no kid anymore, but you need to take responsibility for your New Prosperity, which won't happen if you use credit cards unwisely. One card will serve all of your needs if it's accepted everywhere (most Visas and MasterCards are). Throw out and pay off all department and discount store cards that are exclusive to one merchant. The rates on these cards are sky-high—usually above 20% annually. The best use of a credit card is to pay off the balance by the end of the grace period—usually twenty-five days. That's a responsible use of credit. Paying finance charges does not enhance your life one iota.

- **Make your credit card pay for itself.** If you do have a card that has an annual fee—and it's better not to—make it work for you. There are a host of rebate cards issued by General Motors, Ford, Discover, American Airlines, United Airlines, GE, and many others that will pay you back based on a percentage of the purchases on your cards. If you know you'll be buying a car from a particular manufacturer, put all of your purchases on the card. If you want free airfare, choose an airline card. My wife and I have put all of our personal and business expenses on one card (American AAdvantage) and have not paid for an airline trip in four years. The problem is finding the time to cash in the "miles." If you choose these cards, pay the balance off each month.

- **Get the best terms you can on one credit card.** No-fee, low-interest cards are the best. You can find them on the Internet through RAM Research (800-344-7714) or by calling Bankcard Holders of America (703-389-5445). Of course, for the best rates, you'll need a good credit record. That means you will have to make steady payments on all of your obligations. Always pay your bill on time to avoid late-payment and over-the-credit-limit charges. If you like the services provided by a rebate card, make it the one and only card you use.

LATE-STARTER TIP

You can easily avoid credit traps by choosing the terms of credit you want. First, don't accept any credit offers through junk mail. The terms are often exorbitant or last only a short time. Second, shop around and decide when you can pay off your debt. Set money aside every month for this purpose.

A Quick Way of Auditing Your Debt Load

I know this has an ominous sound to it, but let's have one final look at your debt situation. Let's use a really simple checklist and make it painfully obvious how you are doing:

Mortgage or rent per month _____

Food _____

Utilities _____

Insurance _____

Property taxes _____

Car payments/leases _____

Other essentials _____

1. Essentials subtotal _____

2. Nonessentials (dining, clothing, etc.) _____

3. Monthly net income (minus taxes) _____

Subtract 1 from 3. What's left over? Does 2 (nonessentials) exceed the difference between income and essentials? Are you going into debt to pay for nonessentials? If you are, you need to take a serious look at what you're spending money on. Does it add value to your life? Would you rather be investing this money for your future New Prosperity?

Sensible Insurance

You need insurance, but probably not as much as agents suggest. Certain kinds of policies are more important than others. First, here are a few guidelines that may save you money immediately for your late-start investment plan:

- **If you have no dependents, you need no life insurance.** More specifically, unless your significant other or children will be destitute upon your untimely passing, life insurance is a waste of money. Life insurance is a safety net for the sole provider. It covers any future expenses you're likely to incur if the breadwinner isn't around. So a policy sold to empty nesters who have meaningful assets (home, pension, future Social Security payments) is money that could be spent on retirement.

- **Life insurance is not a retirement plan.** Several leading insurers have run afoul of state regulators and have been forced to return tens of millions in premium dollars for selling life insurance "retirement plans." So beware. Better vehicles come in the form of 401(k)s, 403(b)s, IRAs, Keoghs, and similar plans. Life insurance policies soak you for commissions, fees, and other expenses. You can obtain the money you put into a policy through a loan at a later date, but the rules are complicated and you are better served elsewhere. If you have a policy and no dependents, cash it in and invest it. Obtain a loan from the policy if that's more favorable. If you need life insurance, price a low-cost fixed-premium *term* plan through a no-load broker (see below). Buying whole-life, universal, universal-variable, and similar policies will only enrich the insurer and agent. Don't do it.

- **You'll need a disability plan more than life insurance.** The odds that you will become disabled and lose income far outweigh those of you dying before your time. Most companies offer a disability plan. If not, you can buy them fairly inexpensively through brokers (see below). This is insurance that you need to have—even more so than life insurance.

- **You can save money on homeowners' and auto insurance by raising deductibles.** If you have an older car or can afford a higher out-of-pocket expense, raise those deductibles and watch your premiums drop from 10% to 30%. For example, if you have a vehicle five years old or more, you may want to drop the comprehensive portion of the policy and raise the collision deductibles to $500 or $1,000. Ask your insurer for the value of your vehicle. You may be able to drop collision coverage, too, if the car's mileage exceeds 120,000 miles and it's seven years older or more. This is not a hard-and-fast rule, however. If you don't care about fixing up your vehicle after a fender bender, don't bother with collision coverage. The same goes for your home insurance. Can you afford to take a hit of $500 to $1,000? Invest the savings if you can. Go with a deductible in the amount you can afford to self-insure out of pocket. With both policies, however, make sure to purchase enough coverage to replace all the contents of your home and the full market value of your vehicle. If you live in an especially litigious area, you also should ask

your agent about a $1 million um-
brella liability policy. Then if somebody sues you for big bucks, you're
covered.

Other Sources of Savings/Cash for Your Late-Start Plan

- **Check your property-tax bill and assessment.** Errors are common. If your
assessment says you have a three-car
garage and a four-bedroom home and
you have only a two-car garage and
three bedrooms, you can appeal the assessment and get a reduction in your property-tax bill. If this applies to you, check with
your county or township assessor's office for the appeal process.
Everything must be documented in writing. Mistakes cost you
money, but you can easily correct them.

- **Always look for no-fee/no-load mutual funds, credit cards, and
insurance policies.** That means you pay no commission up front.
Be careful about other fees, however. Obtain and carefully read a
complete disclosure statement.

- **Adjust your employment withholding tax every year.** But don't
trust the IRS's worksheet. Go to an accountant. If you are getting
a refund, you are providing the government with an interest-free
loan for a year or so. If you underwithhold, you pay.

- **Use automatic withdrawal to channel excess funds into a
money market account and to pay bills.** You'll save on postage
and automatically save money. You can also use this feature to automatically invest in investment funds.

- **Don't lease your vehicle unless you can deduct it for business.**
Unfortunately, there are no simple guidelines on leasing. It's a
complex transaction that almost always favors the dealer by lim-
iting mileage and the value of your vehicle at the end of the lease.
You shouldn't be hoodwinked by the "low monthly payment"

come-on of leasing, either. You are paying mostly finance charges for something you are unlikely to own. Leasing definitely won't work if you drive more than 15,000 miles a year or whatever the lease caps the annual mileage at, so it's important to know how much you drive every year. If you have a monster commute, then buy the most reliable vehicle with the best gas mileage. It's better to buy the car and then have something to sell. Leasing is fine if you never want to own the vehicle or constantly want a new set of wheels under warranty every three years or so. You'll almost always have a vehicle under warranty, which means most major repairs are covered. Also, don't be misled by the idea that you can upgrade to a less-energy-efficient vehicle because the monthly payments are lower than buying it. You'll pay more in the long run in fuel costs.

- **Save money on vehicles by buying used, demonstrator, or "program" vehicles or through brokers.** I've done all of the above. The last used car I bought—a 1986 Acura Integra—lasted for 188,000 miles. I bought my present car through a broker and saved $2,000 on the purchase price. A program car has been driven by the dealer or executive and has been well maintained. Cars coming off leases are also good buys and have solid maintenance records.

- **Avoid prepaid funerals.** These will tie up your money for a long time in an overpriced arrangement that is unlikely to keep pace with inflation. Put money aside in your own bank account or separate fund for future expenses. This will save your family the often-exorbitant cost of your funeral.

- **Avoid variable annuities.** These are insurance products bundled with mutual funds. Because of the high commissions and administrative fees, you are almost always better inside a conventional tax-deferred retirement vehicle like a company plan or IRA coupled with a no-load mutual fund.

- **Get overdraft protection for your checking account.** This is actually a small line of credit that covers you in case of accidental overdrafts. It beats paying a $15 or $25 per-check fee, but you have to pay it off immediately when it's used. Otherwise this can cost as much as a credit-card debt.

- **If you are doing home-improvement projects, get fixed-price contracts and estimate dates for completion.** I'm an expert on this. Even the simplest jobs can double in cost if you don't lock in the price. Never pay by the hour, get less than two estimates, take the lowest bidder, or choose a contractor who hasn't done what you want done. Pay only one-third up front and the rest upon completion. If the contractor wants the bulk of his money, he'll do the job right.

- **Simple home energy improvements will save you money on utility bills.** The two biggest consumers of power in your home are your heating/air conditioning unit and your refrigerator. Make sure both are maintained and in good working order. That means getting an annual checkup for the furnace, replacing filters at least every other month, and installing an inexpensive digital thermostat that allows you to set back temperatures when you're asleep or not home. If either appliance is fifteen years old or older, replace it when you can. Today's appliances are from 60% to 80% more efficient than their predecessors. Cheap ways of saving on energy costs include caulking windows to seal leaks, installing chimney-top dampers (to prevent heat loss when a fireplace or woodstove is not in use), adding insulation in the attic, and installing halogen or compact fluorescent light fixtures throughout your home.

- **Plant and maintain a garden.** You can freeze or dry vegetables and enjoy them during the cold months. If you're concerned about the pesticides in produce, grow organic. As Jim Nollman notes in *Spiritual Ecology*, "Gardening has a power that is political as well as democratic. It can be applied constantly, whereas one can only vote occasionally." In fact, of all of my money-saving suggestions in this chapter, this is the one that can afford you the most control in a satisfying way.

Dealing with Brokers

This is perhaps the simplest of all late-start guidelines. First, *never* rely on brokers of any kind to give you financial planning advice. Their compensation is based on how much they sell you, not how well their investments or policies perform. The best use of a broker is to conduct a transaction for you at the lowest possible cost. That means no loads or commissions and you don't pay for their marketing expenses. On stock transactions and real estate deals you can negotiate commissions. Nothing is fixed and the competition is fierce. Check out *The Wall Street Journal* or *Barron's* for the cheapest stock commissions.

Insurance Brokers

Call these companies for term life, universal, disability, or long-term care policies.

Company	Telephone No. (800)
Insurance Quote Services	972-1102
LifeRates	81-RATES
MasterQuote	337-LIFE
Quotesmith	556-9393
SelectQuote	343-1985
Jack White	622-3699

Summary: Ways to Be Savvy and Grow Your New Prosperity Plan

1. See what you can save by prepaying your mortgage principal or refinancing.

2. Save on your transportation expenses by buying the vehicle you need for the lowest price available either by buying used or by going through a broker.

3. Cut down all forms of debt in every way possible.

4. Save on other expenses by purchasing smartly.

5. Use brokers to save money on low-cost, no-commission investment products.

CHAPTER 6

Employing Your Company Retirement Plans

How to Get the Best Returns Out of Your Company Retirement Plans or Start One Up if You Don't Have One

"Those who find others defective, should in themselves dwell reflective."

Julie Jason works in the corporate trenches. As a lawyer and financial adviser, she has to be able to communicate to companies how they can best sell their company retirement plans to their employees, which isn't always an easy task. Despite the fact that the new-style pension plans give employees an unprecedented amount of control over their investments, not all employees take advantage of that.

Julie has a simple message: Get into a retirement plan for growth. By growth, she means growth of capital, not growth of income. Unless you have fewer than five years until retirement, growth will get you where you want to be. As we mentioned earlier, growth often comes from investing in stocks because stocks have the best long-term record of any financial vehicle. Unfortunately, employees don't really start pouring money into company retirement plans until they feel uncomfortable about not having saved enough. There's also the specter of inflation; though it has diminished in the past fifteen years, it still erodes the future value of your money. Only growth investments will tame inflation.

"The one and only reason to participate in a company plan is for growth and to be diversified so you're not afraid of market corrections," Julie advises.

How Defined-Contribution Plans Work

Before the era of the defined-contribution plan, defined-benefit (DB) plans were the dominant company retirement vehicles. Complex and not available to all employees, DB plans paid benefits only if an employee was with a company at least twenty years. Monthly retirement benefits were based on years of service and average income. In other words, you didn't qualify to receive benefits in a DB plan until you were vested—had served a minimum employment period. DB plans thrived in big industrial companies because many employees worked at least thirty years for the same company. If you left the company, the benefits didn't follow you because you often weren't vested. You also had absolutely no control over the money you or your employer invested. It was typically pooled with other employees' funds in huge pension funds and invested conservatively in blue-chip stocks, bonds, and real estate.

With the advent of defined-contribution plans, employees gained more control. Not only do you now have a choice of independently managed mutual funds with these vehicles, but you can allocate money to more than one fund on a percentage basis. The big decisions are now up to you.

Defined-contribution plans also split the responsibility of funding the plan between the employer and the employee. Employees can participate fully or not contribute any money at all. Under profit-sharing plans, employers match employee contributions with a percentage of profits. With more choices than ever before, though, employees balked at the plans at first. Many chose not to, mostly due to their lack of knowledge about investing. There are so many positive reasons to invest in a company plan, it's hard to believe that companies don't spend more time and money educating their employees concerning retirement plans. In addition to health care, it's a prime fringe benefit. Here's why defined-contribution plans work to your advantage:

A Fab Fringe:
Benefits from a Defined-Contribution Plan

Advantage	How You Use It
Pretax contributions	Your contributions are deducted directly from your paycheck, so there is less income to be taxed. That means your contribution is 100% invested. Outside of a plan, a $1,000 investment would have to earn an additional $333 before it would equal your pretax contribution, since that is what the government will take in taxes.
Matching contributions	Your employer will match your pretax contribution, giving you an instant return that you didn't even have to invest. Some companies will match your contribution 100% on the first 3% to 6% of *your* investment. That's a 100% return before you even start.
Flexibility	There are usually a number of mutual funds for you to choose from.
Loan provisions	The larger plans permit you to take out a loan from the plan, although it's always a good idea to leave the money alone unless you have an emergency. There are also "hardship" provisions that allow you to take out money for severe illness and other devastating expenses.
Updated information	The best plans allow you to find out how much your money is growing on a daily

basis through a toll-free number. There are even options that let you transfer between funds on the telephone. You now have more control over your money than ever before. Some funds even allow you to monitor your portfolio on a daily basis through the miracle of voice mail.

Rapid vesting

Most companies permit vesting within one year. That beats waiting ten to twenty years under a defined-benefit plan.

The money is yours

When you leave the company, you can either take your money with you or leave it in the plan. It's yours plus any gains and reinvested capital minus any funds not vested. You can also roll over the funds into another tax-deferred plan when you leave the company or cash it out (and pay a whopping tax bill if you are younger than 59½).

Better managers

Modern plans provide the best independent mutual fund managers available or managers within major fund families such as Fidelity, Vanguard, T. Rowe Price, and many others. It's possible to get the services of a top, market-beating manager if your company offers leading funds.

Regular statements

With the older defined-benefit plans, there were no statements until you retired. Proper 401(k) plans issue statements telling you how much you've invested, what your returns are, and what your money is invested in and for how long. You can track your money as often as every day.

Power of compounding — Not only are your pretax contributions added to those of your company, any investment gains are reinvested automatically. So your compounding power is quadrupled when you consider the tax-deferred nature of the plans.

How Much Should You Invest?

As much as you can. Max out your plan with the highest possible contribution. The chart on page 129 shows how much you can gain from a hypothetical $100 invested over eighteen years with reasonable rate-of-return assumptions.

Types of Plans

With the recent expansion of retirement plans, there's no reason not to have one and benefit from the tax-deferred compounding of what you invest. Not only do the basic requirements of these plans differ from those of traditional retirement plans from ten years ago, but so do the terms of the plans. The newest individual retirement accounts (IRAs), for example, are more flexible and will allow you to contribute even if your employer has a plan offering you the option to pull money out if you need it to pay off education expenses. You'll still have to pay taxes on the funds, however.

IRAs are only vehicles, however. It's how you fuel them that makes a difference in the long term. You can invest in individual stocks, bonds, real estate funds, or mutual funds that invest in nearly any financial instrument. Since you're starting late, the most important characteristic of any investment you choose is carefully sustained growth. Although in chapters 7, 8, and 9

LATE-STARTER TIP

You may have a company plan available to you but not be aware of it or not participate in it, according to the Employee Benefit Research Institute. Of workers eligible to participate in 401(k)s, less than half are contributing the maximum amounts. If you want to reach your New Prosperity goals in a short period of time, you can't afford not to take advantage of these plans and save the maximum allowed.

WHAT $100 A MONTH CAN DO...

This chart summarizes the progress of a hypothetical $100 investment made at the beginning of each month at an assumed 8% rate of return, compounded monthly. All dividends and capital gains have been reinvested and no adjustment has been made for income taxes. These results should not be considered representative of the future performance of any particular investment.

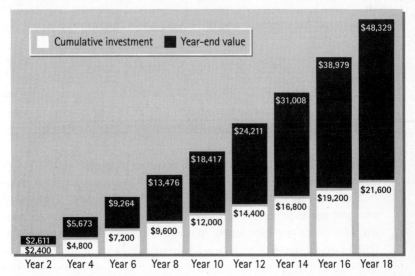

In this example, you have invested a total of $21,600 over eighteen years. Your retirement account has grown to $48,329.

SOURCE: Investment Company Institute

I'll discuss this in more detail, carefully sustained growth is consistent growth of capital that is not unnecessarily risky. Vehicles that do carry unnecessary risks include commodities, stock options, index options, and futures. While the returns on these investments may sound good—especially in radio ads or infomercials—they are not for you. See the chapters on mutual funds, stocks, and income investments for steady growth vehicles you can place within IRAs with confidence.

The array of retirement vehicles open to the general public has never been as diverse as it is today thanks to an explosion of new tax laws (courtesy of the 1997 balanced budget laws) and employers moving to lower-cost, more flexible defined-contribution plans. As mentioned earlier, defined-contribution plans will continue to dominate retirement investing well into the next century as the control over these products shifts from employers to employees. The days of a fixed monthly pension, outside of Social Security, will be an anachronism in the twenty-first century. That's why you need to understand each vehicle and the investments that make it up.

The Differences Between Plans

As a rule, the larger the company you work for, the greater the variety of retirement vehicles it's bound to offer. The following plans are the vehicles most commonly offered by larger employers.

401(k) Plans. Named after a once-obscure section of the U.S. Tax Code, the 401(k) combines pretax payroll withdrawals with separate mutual funds. You tell your company to deduct a specified amount per paycheck and those funds are deposited into mutual funds that are independently managed. Unlike the traditional defined-benefit pension plans usually controlled and managed by employers, 401(k) plans employ mutual fund managers outside the company. The pretax funds reduce your taxable income and are invested on a tax-deferred basis. The funds are also all yours. You can withdraw the money, often get loans from your plan, and roll the funds over into another fund or tax-deferred account when you leave the company or retire. Most companies will match your contribution dollar for dollar up to the first 5% of your salary. If you earn $30,000 a year and your company matches 5%, you end up saving $3,000 per year. So you get 100% return on your contribution before it's even invested in the mutual funds. Talk about found money you don't have to save! Take advantage of that. Most 401(k)s are terrific deals for employees, but only if you keep your money in the plan and invest prudently. As with IRAs, with 401(k)s you are penalized (10% surtax plus income tax) if you withdraw funds before age 59½ unless you can prove a hardship, such as severe illness or education expenses. Although nonprofits generally offer 403(b) plans (see below), 401(k)s can also be offered by tax-exempt organizations. Variations on 401(k) or defined-contribution plans that defer your earnings and invest pretax dollars include thrift plans and company stock plans or employee stock ownership plans. Again, these packages allow you to save pretax dollars and reduce your taxable income and almost always include a matching amount from your company. Don't hesitate to fully fund this plan now.

403(b)s. Named for yet another charming section of the tax code, this provision is essentially the same as a 401(k) only it is available only for nonprofit institutions. Schools, universities, hospitals, charitable groups, and other nonprofits offer these plans to their employees. The same rules that pertain to 401(k)s apply, including the generality that the bigger the institution you work for, the more choices you will most likely have within the mutual funds.

SEP Plans. Tailored for small businesses, sole proprietors, and the self-employed, these simplified IRAs provide most of the benefits of their larger cousins but with a fraction of the paperwork, cost, and administration. With 401(k)s, for example, you may need accountants to pour over the requirements of the plan and a third-party administrator to handle the payroll deductions and transfer funds to the mutual fund managers. With SEPs, however, you simply send your contribution in to a mutual fund firm directly. The paperwork is simple, only a few pages. I set one up myself, and I'm no accountant. The SEP is less flexible, however. If one is offered, it must be offered to all full-time employees and it is funded only through employer contributions.

SIMPLE IRAs. A more advanced product for small companies, the SIMPLE is a more recent innovation that provides 401(k)-type features like payroll deductions with slightly more paperwork than the SEP. There's also more administration, but it may be a good choice for companies employing a hundred employees or fewer. Unlike the 401(k), the SIMPLE doesn't have stringent requirements that all employees must be offered the plan and there's a lot less paperwork.

Keoghs. The grand old man of small-business plans, Keoghs allow for several types of employee contributions, but require a lot of paperwork. Generally they are not used as much anymore because the SIMPLE and SEP plans are easier to start and administer.

Your Own Plans

Until recently, if your company didn't offer a retirement plan, your options were limited. The basic IRA was a simple vehicle, but was extremely limited in its scope and contribution limits. You could use it only for retirement, and if one spouse had a company plan, your contributions and deductions were limited based on income. A revolution has come to personal retirement investing recently, however. Whether you are an independent home-based worker or someone running a shop employing less than a hundred workers, you can set up your own plan. Every mutual fund and brokerage firm will provide the expertise, paperwork, and investment management skills you need to run a successful personal plan.

Even if you haven't contemplated or seeded a retirement plan, the tax laws are full of incentives to get you to start one. The following incentives can get your New Prosperity plan off the ground tomorrow.

Spousal IRAs. Limited in previous years to a $2,250 annual total contribution, spousal IRAs were expanded last year by Congress by allowing contributions up to $4,000 per year or not more than $2,000 per each spouse's account. You can contribute even if one spouse doesn't work. These are not as tax-advantaged as 401(k)/403(b)/SIMPLE plans because you are contributing *post-tax* dollars, but they are a good option if you've fully funded all of your other retirement vehicles—or don't have any at the present time.

Penalty-Free IRA Withdrawals. This is not a plan, but an emergency provision that may protect your other retirement savings. Say you have an expensive surgery or condition that forces you to incur thousands of dollars in unreimbursed medical expenses. The expenses exceed 7.5% of your adjusted gross income, which is your income minus all deductions such as mortgage interest, property taxes, and miscellaneous expenses. This type of withdrawal covers only out-of-pocket medical expenses that exceed the 7.5% threshold. You can take money out of your IRA to cover the medical expenses without incurring the 10% surtax. There's also a break on the withdrawal surtax if you've been unemployed and receiving unemployment for at least twelve consecutive weeks. The withdrawals can then be used to pay for medical insurance premiums. If you're also stuck paying college bills, you get to pass on the surtax to pay for "qualified higher education expenses for yourself, spouse, child or grandchild." That break applies to tuition and related fees, but not room and board. These new rules also emerged from the 1997 budget bill.

Roth IRAs. Also called "The American Dream" IRA, this is one of the newest IRAs built into the 1997 tax code. Although the contributions you make to it are not tax deductible, you can make tax-free withdrawals without penalty if you invest the money for at least five years and you're older than 59½ when you take the withdrawals. You're limited to $2,000 per year if your income is under $160,000 for couples and $110,000 for singles. You can also pull money out to buy a home or pay for qualified education expenses (tuition and fees, but not room and board) as long as you hold the money for at least five years. This vehicle is a worthwhile supplement to other plans you have. It's a great deal for those with more than a decade to retirement. But always fully fund your pretax or deductible plans first.

HOPE Education Credits. If there's one great impediment to funding retirement plans, it's paying big college bills. If educational expenses are still a financial burden at this point in your life, there are ways of reducing that load under the current tax laws. While the new provisions won't actually pay the bills, they'll give you some useful tax credits along the way. You can obtain a $1,500 HOPE Scholarship credit for the first two years of post-secondary education for yourself, a spouse, or your children. You are allowed to use this only for tuition, fees, and books, not room and board, and you are not eligible if you make more than $100,000 in adjusted gross income filing jointly and $50,000 filing singly per year. If you are not allowed to claim the HOPE credit, anyone can write off up to 20% of tuition and related expenses up to $10,000. The same income limits apply.

Your Own Plans: A Mini-Review

The best strategy with the new IRAs for late-starters is to

- Fully fund all 401(k), 403(b), or SIMPLE plans with pretax money.

- Know how much you can contribute to your company plans. For 1998, the maximum elective deferral is $10,000 per year for 401(k)s and 403(b)s.

- Supplement your company plans with deductible contributions to your own/spousal IRAs, if you qualify.

- Contribute to your existing IRAs even if you don't qualify for the deductions.

- Set up the most appropriate IRA or pension plan if you don't have anything.

- Use growth stock mutual funds providing lower-than-average risk and superior returns to beat inflation and fund your New Prosperity plan.

Diversifying and Getting Maximum Return

Many companies don't realize that employees often go into heavy denial when choosing funds from a retirement plan. Many believe they are not saving enough or think they aren't picking the right vehicles. It's simple, however, to pick the right mix of funds if you understand diversification. When you diversify, you spread your risk around by allocating your funds among several different types of investments. Under this principle, you divide your money up to ensure investment success.

If you are investing on your own, you may have noticed that there are some 6,000 mutual funds from which to choose. Anxiety often leads many to invest nothing; that's not an option at this point in your late-start plan. Diversification is what you want. A diversified plan provides you some degree of protection when markets, industries, or continental/regional economies go sour. Large-company stocks may not move in the same direction as small-company stocks. Stocks with dividends will withstand the storms of the market better than those without. And it always pays to have some money in overseas markets, which move differently than domestic markets. In other words, there is safety in variety.

Diversification is a proven method of safely enhancing your returns over time. Diversification is the standard practice in professional investment management. As an individual investor, you can enjoy the same advantages. When you are offered the menu of funds through your plan—or are choosing them for your own plan—there are some standard offerings that will start you on your way in diversification.

How you choose to diversify depends on how long you have to invest. If you have fifteen years in which to invest, keep it simple and charge ahead. Put 20% in each of the following: growth/large-cap, growth/small-cap, value, index, and international. Or put 60% in growth or aggressive growth funds and 40% in either growth/equity-income or index funds. This is the "pedal to the metal" portfolio. The following are your basic allocation options:

STAPLES OF YOUR PORTFOLIO: FUND TYPES AND ALLOCATION

Type	Securities Held	Suggested Allocation %
Growth/large-cap	Large companies	Large/more than 60%
Growth/mid-cap	Medium-sized companies	Medium/20%
Growth/small-cap	Aggressive smaller companies	Medium

Type	Securities Held	Suggested Allocation %
Value (all sizes)	Stocks selling at a discount	Medium
Growth/income	Stocks with high dividends	Small/less than 10%
Balanced	Mixture of stocks and bonds	Small
Index	Largest 500 stocks	Large
International	Overseas funds	No more than 25%
Income	Bonds and high-dividend stocks	Small
GIC	Fixed-income contract	None
Money market	Low-yield securities	None

How to Spread Risk Around

Generally, the more risk you take, the higher your potential for return. In addition to total return, ask your fund managers for the beta of each fund. This is a measurement of how much risk you are taking relative to an index of the 500 largest stocks. A beta of 1.00 means you are taking the same amount of risk as an index fund that contains the 500 largest stocks on the New York Stock Exchange, also called the Standard & Poor's 500 index. A beta of 1.25 suggests you're in for 25% more risk than the market averages. And the measure works the other way for reduced risk.

If you're looking at a ten- to fifteen-year investment period, stick with 25% in an index fund, 25% in a growth/small-cap fund, 25% in an international fund, and 25% in a balanced fund. Those with less than ten years should consider 25% in an index fund, 25% in a balanced fund, 25% in an international fund, and 25% in an income fund. Of course, these are just suggested allocations. Keep in mind that you don't need to have more than 25% in a type of fund. And forget about money market funds within a company plan.

They are a wasted opportunity. Money market funds track the lowly U.S. Treasury Bill rate. Sure, these are safe funds in that your principal never declines, but what you need is growth, which money funds don't offer.

Summary: Your Company Plan Is an Easy Route to New Prosperity

1. Fully fund all existing company plans with pretax dollars.

2. If you don't have a company plan, start one and fully fund it.

3. Know what plans do and how they work for you.

4. Diversify within company plans. Don't put all of your money into one fund or stock.

5. Go for growth.

CHAPTER 7

Marathoners in Mutual Funds

How to Choose the Best Mutual Funds for Growth

"You can observe a lot by watching."

—Yogi Berra

Like you, I'm something of a late bloomer. I didn't hit puberty until I was 19. I got married at 30. I became a parent at 40. Consequently, I didn't get really serious about most things in life until well into my fifth decade. Fortunately, you can make up for lost time. My wife and I have had success in picking mutual funds. We should've done well. I've had access to some of the best information on investing in the world over the past ten years, with subscriptions to *Barron's, The Wall Street Journal, The New York Times, Money, Kiplinger's Personal Finance, Worth, Smart Money, Business Week, Forbes, Morningstar Mutual Funds,* and many other newsletters. Not only did I read every issue of these publications during the last decade, I freelanced for *Barron's* and knew the gentlemen who started Morningstar, the premier mutual-fund rating service, which provided me with information on all their top-rated funds for free. I also attended every annual Morningstar conference, heard and interviewed the most brilliant mutual fund managers of our time, and attended one major investing conference per year.

I once shared a dais with Ralph Wanger, who manages the Acorn Fund. Ralph is a legend in the business, since Acorn has a superb twenty-year-plus record. Since Ralph's forte is small-company stocks, he's used the acorn moniker—"from tiny acorns mighty oaks grow"—for his flagship fund and two newer funds, Acorn USA and Acorn International. Morningstar had asked me to fill in as a panel conference moderator for another journalist who couldn't make it. The conference up until that point had been, well, rather dull. Managers were tediously presenting sales pitches for their funds, although they are asked to explain their stock and bond picks. So I thought I'd liven things up.

At the time, Vice President Dan Quayle was all the rage for underperforming intellectually in his role as "one heartbeat away from the president." He did wonderful things like correct children in their spelling of *potato* (preferring the Middle English spelling *potatoe*). So I thought I'd make a joke in front of a crowded Hyatt ballroom of money managers, investors, and other conference attendees. "Dan Quayle was recently speaking at the United Negro College Fund," I began, "where their motto is 'A mind is a terrible thing to waste.' But our vice president thought better of it and revised it to 'What a terrible thing it is not to have a mind.' "

Instead of hearty laughter, I heard the distinct, unmistakable roar of the air-conditioning system. Not only had I managed to offend every Republican money manager in the room, but unbeknownst to me, the vice president himself was to speak in that very room later that evening during a GOP fund-raiser. Talk about inappropriate! I was fortunate that some guys talking into their sleeves didn't wrestle me to the ground. Even more fortunate was that Wanger was hilarious and provided some solid investment advice. The moral here: You can do something very inappropriate in society—and investing—if you don't think about it first. I thought my Quayle joke was clever; it wasn't. Fortunately, my panel and I were much more adept at investment advice. It's a big world out there, especially when it comes to mutual funds. If you don't know what you're doing, all the humor in the world won't make up for lost time and lost investment gains.

Mutual Funds Do the Dirty Work for You

Mutual funds are ideal vehicles for middle- to long-term investors because they will follow one investment philosophy—their objective—and stick with it no matter what the market does. You want to concentrate on growth as an objective. You can gain growth half a dozen ways in mutual funds. You can invest in small companies, overseas companies, companies that are underpriced relative to their peers, or big companies with healthy dividends. There are hundreds of funds that pursue growth as an objective, but few that do it consistently well. It's a lot easier to choose the wrong funds than the ones that will perform over time.

I initially did all the wrong things when I invested in mutual funds. I bought last year's winners, daredevils that were good for only a few quarters of growth and funds that had their best years behind them. We also got bombed like most everyone else in the 1987 crash—and pulled out at the wrong time. During the autumn decline of 1997, we learned our lesson and didn't move a dime out of the market, which recovered quickly. After the 1987 crash, I discovered that "buy low, sell high" applied only partially to mutual funds. The key is "buy low, and if there's quality management, stay put." That's how you make money, but you have to find *marathon* mutual funds that can outrun the market's worst excesses. These are funds that keep on running when most of their peers are gasping for air. These funds will also go the distance and can help counter the fact that you have only a short time to invest. You build a portfolio around these long-distance runners and they'll pound the pavement and sweat for you.

The best funds do the thankless job of staying in the market when others are bailing out—and making money during the market's rebound. They also invest in specialized industries that have excellent potential over the next twenty years. If you're a big believer in technology, health care, and financial services, you can find funds that will invest in companies that cater to those needs. If you want a broad-based index fund that just invests in the 500 largest companies in the stock market, you can find several funds fitting that description as well. In fact, for most people, an index fund is the lowest cost, highest-performing way of beating the majority of stock mutual funds. Through 1997, Standard & Poor's stock index funds beat most managed mutual funds over the last five years.

More important, the only way to beat inflation—your greatest investment enemy—is to invest in growth stocks. These stocks produce rising profits every year and easily outpace bonds, CDs, and money market funds, which don't beat inflation. Mutual funds corral these stocks to help you achieve at least 10% per year in average returns.

If you're starting late in your retirement plan, you can do your investment planning yourself. It's a lot of work, but there's no doubt you can do it if you so desire. Time is of the essence, however. You want to be on some beach chasing grandkids in ten to twenty years. There are mutual funds that can get you on that beach. Most people just don't have the time to research hundreds of stocks and bonds. These carefully chosen funds are the vehicles that can take you to your destination, but you need to understand how they work and take action to make them part of your investment plan.

Even if you haven't been able to save a dime for your retirement, it's not too late. Mutual funds can be part of IRAs, set up to receive automatic withdrawals from your checking account, and are the mainstays of 401(k)s and 403(b)s. Don't be meek about this need to go for growth. Even in 401(k) pension plans—where long-time employees can afford to take risks in tax-deferred mutual funds—a survey found that a meager 6% of those polled invested in stocks, according to Hewitt Associates. Less than 2% of employee funds went into aggressive growth or international stock funds, which have the best combined records over time. That's why you may need to take the time to learn about fund objectives and how they can achieve your retirement goals faster.

As investment pools that employ professional managers, funds fall into three camps: poor, average, and exceptional. Unfortunately, most choose funds from the first two because they don't do their research. Let's face it, you have little time to put up with a loser. With the astounding variety of 6,000 funds to choose from, you can find great growth vehicles. But you have to know what kind of fund you need before you send in your money. Some funds are clearly better than others and some excel in specialties, such as international and small-cap investing. You don't have access to the kind of research they do. That's why it pays to add them to your portfolio to diversify and reduce risk.

How Funds Work

Most mutual funds are open-ended, meaning that every time new money comes in, they create new shares for new investors. When investors cash in their shares, fund managers issue redemptions. The fund price is determined by the average of all of the stocks owned divided by the number of shares. This is known as the net asset value (NAV), which is the number listed in the business section of your newspaper. When the shares of the stocks held by the fund go up in value, so does the NAV. That means your holdings rise in value, which is calculated by multiplying the number of shares you own times the current NAV.

Stock fund managers generally follow several camps. The most aggressive stay in the market all the time or are fully invested no matter what. Their more conservative counterparts will retreat to cash in the form of U.S. Treasury securities or money market instruments if they think a decline is imminent. Since most managers and amateurs alike guess wrong on the direction of the market, for your purposes, it's best to stay with a manager who's fully invested at all times.

Closed-end mutual funds, by contrast, issue a fixed number of shares and trade like a stock on exchanges. You buy shares through brokers and figure your performance based on market value and net asset value (NAV)—the average of all securities prices divided by the number of shares outstanding. Although there are plenty of good ones, I'm not recommending any closed-end funds because it's difficult to tell if you are getting a good price and you must buy them through a broker and pay a commission.

Open-ended mutual funds only figure performance based on NAV. Unlike their open-ended brethren, closed-end funds hold on to their positions as long as they like. Redemptions are made by trading shares on a stock exchange. Although there are only a handful of closed-end funds, they allow managers more freedom and specialization. They include everything from bond funds to single-country funds. Generally, though, you're better off in open-ended mutual funds because there are more of them and you can buy them without paying a stockbroker a commission. No-load funds are commissionless funds that, all other things being equal, will increase your returns. Remember, any fund expenses eat into your returns because they are deducted from what you invest.

What do funds do that you can't do? Well, nothing really, except they can do it in greater volume and efficiency. Every fund employs a staff of analysts who look for the best buys in specific areas. Say you need a fund that specializes in technology stocks because you are particularly uninformed or squeamish in that area. You know that certain technologies will be surging over the next decade, but you don't know the difference between a microprocessor and a food processor. So you're paying for the expertise. Here are some of the specialized fund categories available to you:

Aggressive Growth/Small Company. These are the high-performance sports cars of funds, as they stay invested in stocks all the time for maximum returns and risk. They invest in everything from unproven small companies to earnings-driven blue chips. They are among the riskiest groups in the short term, yet over decades they easily beat all other categories if well managed. These are the best kinds of funds to be in if you have at least ten years to invest until retirement. The more time you have, the more aggressive the fund you can choose because time evens out your overall risk.

Growth. These are stock funds that generally follow companies with consistent earnings growth. Although they usually aren't as risky as aggressive growth funds, they are good choices if you have less than ten years to go or if you just don't want to take on the additional risk of more aggressive growth funds. Index funds that mimic a large group of stocks such as the Standard & Poor's 500 are considered growth funds that employ average risk and have low operating expenses (see below).

Growth and Income/Equity-Income. These combine stocks with healthy dividends and occasionally bonds. These are the most conservative, yield-oriented stock funds. These funds, along with balanced and income funds, provide modest growth in principal with lower risk than the previous two categories. If you have less than five years before you plan to retire, these are lower-risk alternatives to pure growth funds.

Balanced. These funds combine a fixed percentage of stocks and bonds and are for the most conservative equity investors. Again, use these funds only within five years of your retirement. They don't provide much growth, but the diversification lowers your risk.

Income. Bonds of every stripe occupy this niche. They run the gamut from U.S. government obligations to risky corporate junk (high-yield) bonds. Generally avoid these type of funds unless you have a consistent need for income.

International/Global. Also called emerging markets or world funds, these foreign securities vehicles get as specialized as one region (Asia, Europe, etc.) or cover the entire world. These funds should comprise from 10% to 30% of your portfolio. Because they provide you with diversification outside the U.S. markets, that also lowers your overall risk.

Sector. These are the most specialized of fund groups. They often cover single industries (autos, food) or subindustries (biotechnology, software). They are typically subsets of the aggressive growth or small-company funds. You combine these funds with growth funds only if you have at least a decade to invest for a boost in returns.

Money Market. These are classic parking places for cash that emphasize short-term securities at an unchanging $1 per share NAV. There are no capital gains possible from investing in these funds, so they are relatively safe. Don't use them within retirement vehicles. They are ideal for emergency or short-term savings only.

Choosing a Fund Manager

Once you've picked the fund objectives that give you proper diversification (growth/income/international), you need to examine returns. Ideally, the fund(s) you choose should offer consistently above-average returns relative to the risk they're taking. How do you measure this elusive factor? My best suggestion is to consult *Morningstar Mutual Funds* or magazines that feature their ratings. Morningstar and its chief competition *Value Line* evaluate risk, returns, management, and portfolios. They save you a tremendous amount of time and energy by vetting thousands of funds. You, however, still have the make the final decisions as to which funds to choose.

Morningstar uses a star rating system that measures a risk/return ratio. Their highest rating is 5 stars, meaning that the fund performed the best among its group with the least possible amount of risk. To date, this is one of the best measures of fund performance. Morningstar's star system, however, does not guarantee that the fund will perform that well in the future. As every fund is obligated to tell you, past performance is no guarantee of future return.

The reason why I recommend a risk/return rating over pure performance is that you have to take a holistic approach of the fund you're considering. Holistic evaluation involves a similar process to selecting single stocks, only there are more factors to consider. The

---

LATE-STARTER TIP

The closer you are to retirement, the less risk you can take. Those with a decade or more should consider growth/aggressive growth funds. Those with five years or less should consider growth/income/balanced funds. Every portfolio, however, should have growth funds—at least 30%. International funds should also comprise about 20% of your portfolio. Growth beats inflation and international stocks reduce risk through diversification.

following information all fund companies must disclose in in fund documents such as the prospectus:

Performance Periods. Never trust a one-year performance record. The longer the period you have to study, the better. Unfortunately, most funds don't have twenty-year-plus records. So you have to settle for three-, five-, and 10-year records. "Total Return" is the most relevant performance figure because it shows capital gains/losses minus the fund expenses, such as loads.

Yield. If you're seeking income, this is one figure that's important. Most stock funds don't have a high yield because they concentrate on growth, which is what you need more than income.

Loads and Expenses. You're better off not paying any load and the lowest possible expense ratio. Loads are commissions that fund groups extract from your money to pay brokers and salespeople. There are thousands of no-loads that should be your first preference. The expense ratio includes commissions and management fees. Usually, the larger the fund, the lower the expense ratio. Stock funds charging more than 1.50% a year for expenses cost too much. Bond funds should charge half that. Money market funds often waive their management fees.

12b-1 Charges. This is also called a distribution charge, and ranges from .25% to 1.25% of the amount invested annually. These fees, imposed every year, often amount to greater burdens than one-time loads for long-term investors. Avoid funds that charge them. Again, *your* money's tapped to pay for the fund's marketing expenses.

Objective. Although this is often a fuzzy term, it describes how the manager seeks to invest the fund. Some funds target stocks in the health care industry and ignore everything else. Other funds aim for growth from countries in the Asian Pacific region. The objective is one of the most closely monitored sections of a portfolio. If your objectives match those of the management, then this is a key hurdle cleared.

Performance Relative to Objective. This is a key screen that allows you to compare the fund's return relative to similar funds. This "apples-to-apples" comparison gives you a better picture of how the fund did among its peers. Morningstar further measures this number in its "Morningstar risk" figure.

Cash Holdings. The percentage of cash holdings isn't too revealing, but tells you how much of the fund's money is invested in the market. Fully invested funds often are 10% to 20% invested in cash. Pessimistic fund managers, however, retreat to cash when they think the market is due for a downturn. They are, in effect, timing the market, which means most of the time they'll guess wrong on the market's direction.

Sector Weightings. This is another key factor that will determine if you need the fund's expertise. These are percentage allocations in specific industry sectors. These subgroups include natural resources (oil and gas, paper), industrial products (machine tools, equipment), consumer durables (vehicles, appliances), nondurables (food, beverages), retail trade, services, utilities, transportation, finance (banks, insurance), and multi-industry.

Fundamental Analysis. If you really want to get specific and read a manager's mind, you can obtain information on average price/earnings, price/book, and earnings/growth rates.

Style Ratings. What kind of investor is the manager? Does he or she favor growth (earnings) or value (low asset prices)? Does he or she prefer small, medium, or large capitalization companies? Or does he or she seek a blend of all of the above? Morningstar provides this analysis.

Bond Ratings. These factors include averaged weighted maturities, credit quality, duration, weighted prices, and coupons. Essentially, most of these figures tell you how risky the bond portfolio is relative to credit quality and maturity.

Turnover Ratio. This percentage tells you how much of the portfolio is sold off each year. High-turnover funds generate higher expenses that can lower your returns if performance doesn't outweigh the increased trading costs.

Portfolio Manager. While there are some stars in the business, they rarely do well every year and can't do well without a good fund family of analysts behind them. Good managers and families can make new, no-record funds exciting possibilities for our portfolio. You should also note if a fund has changed managers recently. That may be a sign that the fund will be managed differently. In most cases, the best fund families have talented "managers-in-waiting" to take over hot-performing funds.

Market Price and Premium/Discount. For closed-ends only, this indicates the price at which a fund was purchased or sold on a exchange and the difference between the fund's NAV and its market price. A positive number indicates a premium; negative is a discount. While it's generally best to buy at a discount, good funds are all too often bought at a premium. Again, unless you really know what you're doing, avoid these funds.

Alpha and Beta. The alpha is the difference between a fund's actual performance and its expected performance, given its level of risk, which is measured by beta. A negative alpha denotes underperformance. Beta shows how much risk is taken on given the S&P 500's annual performance. A beta of 1.00 equals the market performance of the S&P 500 index. Above 1.00 denotes more risk, below 1.00 denotes less. For example, a beta of 1.10 means the fund should beat the market by 10% in bull markets and drop (at least) 10% in down markets.

What Do You Really Need to Know?

Why pay attention to this mountain of information? To summarize, you need to concentrate on several factors when investing that will match funds to your age and risk tolerance:

1. Do the fund objectives match your needs (growth/income/international)?

2. Do the funds take the kind of risk you're willing to accept?

3. Do the funds produce above-average returns with low to modest expenses?

4. Do the funds provide diversification within your portfolio among large-, midsize, value, international, and small-company stocks?

Making a Marathon Portfolio

You have two choices. You can go out and hand-pick your own funds based on the following criteria or save time by using the recommended funds below. This is a systematic process like assembling a model from a kit. Walk through these steps when deciding on the right fund.

1. **What is your objective?** If you know the objective or category of the fund you need to fill a hole in your portfolio, start with that. Most fund rating services list funds by category, although every service is slightly different. This part of the search demands that you ask "What do I want the fund to do?" Do you want a fund that's invested solely in South America? Do you want a fund that focuses on information technology stocks? Pick an objective or two, seize a handful of fund prospectuses (by calling the toll-free fund hotlines), and make your picks. Since you're starting late, you want to concentrate on growth as an objective.

2. **What is the fund's performance and risk rating?** How did the fund do in up and down markets? How did it fare against funds of similar objectives? How often did it beat the S&P 500 or the Lehman Brothers bond index if you're looking at a bond fund? What is the annual average return for the longest period of time recorded? Was it more or less risk-averse?

3. **How much does it cost?** Does it have an undesirable front-end, back-end, reinvestment, or 12b-1 fee? Does it have an unusually

high expense or turnover ratio? Does it have a high cost of entry? Most funds take minimum investments of $1,000, but some are as high as $50,000 to $100,000.

4. **How consistent is its management?** Have there been frequent changes of managers? How long has the present manager been there? Have new managers changed objectives? Your managers should have the expertise and longevity to be able to spot stocks and trends and be able to profit from them over time. If there's a lot of turnover in fund management, that may suggest trouble.

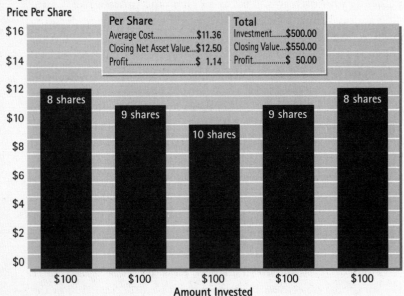

HOW DOLLAR-COST AVERAGING WORKS

Regular investments of $100 purchased a total of 44 shares in this simplified illustration.

Per Share		Total	
Average Cost	$11.36	Investment	$500.00
Closing Net Asset Value	$12.50	Closing Value	$550.00
Profit	$ 1.14	Profit	$ 50.00

In this example, $100 worth of a mutual fund was purchased on a regular basis. As the fund's price fluctuated between $10 and $12.50 a share, more shares were bought as the price declined. In this case, the investor earned a 10% profit although the initial and closing share prices were the same because the average cost was lower than the final value per share.

Marathon Fund Portfolios

If you don't want to do any research, here are a few portfolios of relatively low-cost/high-performance marathon funds that meet my earlier qualifications that are appropriate for the time until you'll need the money for retirement. These are diversified portfolios across countries, industries, and investing styles. If you want mini-versions of each portfolio, just pick the top three funds in each group. Despite my screening, you'll still need to do some homework: Check them every year to see that they're performing as well as or better than their peers using the information I provided earlier in this chapter. All returns are through December 31, 1997.

EARLY BIRD: FIFTEEN YEARS UNTIL RETIREMENT

Fund	Five-Year AAR	Phone (800)
T. Rowe Price International	13.0%	638-5660
Janus	15.8%	525-8983
Third Avenue Value	19.4%	443-1021
Vanguard 500	20.1%	662-7447
Dodge & Cox Stock	21.1%	621-3979
Longleaf Partners	21.4%	445-9469
Vanguard Specialized Health	22.6%	662-7447

CAN DO: TEN TO FIFTEEN YEARS . . .

Fund	Five-Year AAR	Phone
Brandywine	18.4%	656-3017
Janus Worldwide	19.8%	525-8983
Vanguard 500	20.1%	662-7447
Babson Value	20.9%	422-2766
T. Rowe Price Science & Technology	21.1%	638-5660
Mairs & Power Growth	23.7%	304-7404

BETTER LATE THAN NEVER:
FIVE TO TEN YEARS . . .

Fund	Five-Year AAR	Phone
Warburg-Pincus International Equity	11.6%	927-2874
Acorn	17.8%	922-6769
Fidelity Equity- Income II	18.5%	544-8888
Vanguard 500	20.1%	662-7447
Oakmark	22.8%	625-6275
CGM Realty	26.7%*	345-4048

*Equals one-year return. Fund does not have a five-year history, but is worth investing in due to its diversification and management.

LAST CHANCE: FIVE YEARS . . .

Fund	Five-Year AAR	Phone
Strong Government Securities	7.9%	368-1030
Linder Dividend	11.4%	314-727-5305
CGM Mutual	12.8%	345-4048
Dodge & Cox Balanced	16.1%	621-3979
Cohen & Steers Realty	19.1%	437-9912
T. Rowe Price Equity-Income	20.0%	638-5660

Portfolio Notes

If you don't have the means to build a fully diversified portfolio of all of the recommended funds for your situation, choose the first or second fund in each portfolio as a starter. The Vanguard Index 500 fund alone covers the 500 top industrial companies in the United States and typically beats the return of most actively managed stock funds. Its expenses are also among the lowest in the business because the same 500 stocks stay in the portfolio and give you exposure to prime companies such as GE, Microsoft, Procter & Gamble, and Intel.

The closer you are to retirement, the more your portfolio should be aimed at providing you with income, which is why the portfolios nearer to retirement tend to focus on high-dividend stocks, bonds, and real estate. The income component of your portfolio, which is for short-term needs and goals, is contained in chapter 9.

Dollar-Cost Averaging: The Best Way to Ease into Funds and Reduce Risk

Besides compound interest, dollar-cost averaging is going to become one of your best friends as you get into your New Prosperity plan. Dollar-cost averaging is simple: Automatically invest certain amounts of money in the mutual funds (or stocks) of your choices. Send a check in every month. Dollar-cost averaging helps you avoid the big dips or run-ups that are likely to increase your risk of getting into the market at the wrong time. Your average investment over time captures the highs and lows of the market, so you don't have to get anxious about getting in at the right time. For your peace of mind, you should know that numerous studies have proven that market timing doesn't work anyway—even if you are a professional trader.

Dollar-cost averaging reduces your risk because time is on your side. If you've chosen your funds well, your average investment will be worth more in the future. Your cost to purchase new shares varies from time to time, but that's how it works. Say you are investing over a five-month period in a mutual fund. Each month you invest $100, but because the market fluctuates, your money buys more shares in one month and less in the other. If you invest in a range of market conditions—from $10.00 to $12.50 per share, for example—your average cost over the five months is $11.36 per share (see the graph on page 150). That's right in the middle of the share-price range and that's where it's safe to be. In this example, you even make a 10% profit.

You can do this with every fund you own by making automatic withdrawals from savings or checking accounts directly into the funds. It works automatically and you never write a check or miss the money. Better yet, if the money flows out of your short-term accounts (checking/money market/savings) without you touching it, you will adjust your monthly budget accordingly. Because you have this "invisible savings plan," you regularly spend less and invest more.

Fund Group Specialties

Each fund group has specialties. Fidelity, Merrill Lynch, and Vanguard offer a fund for every purpose. Most fund buyers may not know, however, that Vanguard specializes in low management expenses or that nearly every fund offered by a brokerage house is loaded with commissions or fees.

The smaller fund groups have refined specialties. Invesco and T. Rowe Price have excellent "sector" funds that specialize in hot industries. Franklin-Templeton has a stable of aggressive international funds. American Century/Benham has everything from zero-coupon bond funds to aggressive growth funds.

Despite the existence of fund families that encourage you to do one-stop shopping within the family, don't feel locked into one group. You can select among a number of funds in mutual fund networks through discount brokers (see the following page), although in doing so you will pay complex "transactions" fees in addition to management expenses. Of course you can invest in every fund directly unless you are going through a broker, which I think is unnecessary and don't advise.

Salespeople—namely brokers with banks or brokerage houses—will naturally push "their" funds because they earn a commission from each one they sell. Keep in mind that these salespeople offer little or no financial advice for the easy commission they earn. You should avoid any load or "12-b-1" from any family because it eats into your investment return.

The following are some fund groups that have excelled in particular areas. Call for more information.

Fund Groups and Their Specialties

American Century/Benham: Aggressive small company/bonds (800-345-2021)

Calvert: socially responsible growth and income (800-368-2748)

Evergreen: small company growth and income (800-235-0064)

Fidelity: industry sector funds and every other objective (800-544-8888).

Invesco: overseas, sector funds (800-525-8085)

Merrill Lynch: overseas/Pacific Basin (800-637-3863)

Neuberger Berman: growth, income (800-877-9700)

Phoenix: growth and income, income (800-243-4361)

T. Rowe Price: overseas, technology (800-638-5660)

Royce group: small-company value funds (800-221-4268)

Scudder: income, overseas (800-225-2470)

Templeton/Franklin: value and overseas emerging markets (800-292-9293)

Vanguard: Low-cost index, sector, and overseas (800-662-7447)

Fund Resources

Note: These resources should be in your public library. Although there are hundreds of mutual fund resources, these are the best. They can save you a great deal of time in researching the funds you need that will benefit you most. The books and rating services on the following page boil down everything you need to know in an even more succinct way.

Books and Brochures

The Best Mutual Funds in America by Gene Walden (Dearborn, 1997)

Getting Started in Mutual Funds by Alan Lavine (Wiley, 1994)

No-Load Investors Mutual Fund Guide by Sheldon Jacobs

The Mutual Fund Encyclopedia by Gerald Perritt

Investment Company Institute Guide to Mutual Funds (ICI Publications)

Mutual Fund Education Alliance (MFEA Publications)

Mutual Fund Rating Services

Morningstar, 225 W. Wacker Dr., Chicago, IL 60606 (800-876-5005, 312-696-6000, www.morningstar.net) The leading fund-rating service, Morningstar has expanded to cover nearly every aspect of fund investing. Not only does Morningstar provide per-formance analyses, it breaks out tax liabilities, management changes, risk/return numbers, and holdings by industry sector.

The main product, *Morningstar Mutual Funds,* is a constantly updated biweekly newsletter that comes in a binder. Although a bit overwhelming for most individual investors, Morningstar's flagship product is a comprehensive look at the industry, evaluating one to three fund groups every issue. A much more boiled-down version of their information is available in their newsletter *The Five-Star Investor.*

The hallmark of Morningstar's system is its star rating system, which balances risk and return. A 5 in the system would signal a fund with the best possible performance and the lowest relative risk. Every statistical measure of risk, return, and indices is in-cluded in every Morningstar page.

For computer users, Morningstar data is available in a CD-ROM product and programs such as Principia. The software with the data allows you to pose what-if questions, plot your own graphs, and come up with customized fund lists based on any number of criteria (asset size, return, risk, etc.). They also sell software to analyze funds and stocks.

Value Line Mutual Fund Survey, 220 E. 42nd St., New York, NY 10017-5891 (800-284-7607) This newer service looks remarkably like Morningstar, but doesn't feel like it. Although it covers some 2,000 funds, its commentary is not as incisive nor does it perform "tax liability" ratings on the funds that Morningstar performs. They also lack the powerful companion software products.

Like Morningstar, the Value Line product is a binder newsletter with one-page summaries of funds laid out in pretty much the same way. All performance and relative measures are included on every page. One useful feature of Value Line that Morningstar doesn't have yet is an investment planning worksheet that allows you to chart risk and match funds that meet your risk tolerance. They also throw in a monthly newsletter and a book, *How to Invest in Mutual Funds.* Other key sections include market outlook, fund close-ups, fund selectors, news briefs, and performance reviews. Like Morningstar, Value Line is also available on CD-ROM.

Magazine/Newspaper Resources

Every major business and financial newspaper/magazine runs regular coverage on mutual funds. The best coverage is done by:

Barron's

Business Week

Financial World

Forbes

Kiplinger's Personal Finance

Money

Mutual Funds

Smart Money

The Wall Street Journal

Worth

Your Money

Mutual Fund Networks

These fund networks allow you to consolidate all of your records and "trade" between funds through a phone call. Their greatest advantage is selection and convenience. Most of the major networks allow you access to hundreds of funds with one call. All rates and conditions are subject to change. They will, however, require you to be a brokerage customer and charge you "transactions" fees to use the networks.

Fidelity FundsNetwork (800-544-9697) The largest mutual fund group offers funds outside of its own group, which covers more than 300 funds from thirty-two other "families."

Charles Schwab Mutual Fund OneSource (800-266-5623) This is the premier mutual funds network service, offering more than 800 funds. Although you can't get into every fund through this service, it's a good way of avoiding a heap of sales charges. Like the other services, you have a choice of no-transaction-fee (NTF) or transaction-fee funds.

Jack White & Co. (800-323-3263) This deep-discount broker has an impressive funds network and is worth considering to find some of the smaller funds. More than 700 funds from fifty different families are available, with 317 on a NTF basis.

Summary: Finding Marathon Mutual Funds

1. Understand how mutual funds work, their objectives, and the different types to choose from.

2. Pick the best funds for a diversified portfolio or use my picks.

3. Use dollar-cost averaging to make investments every month into the funds of your choice.

4. Use fund resources to shop for and evaluate funds on an on-going basis.

CHAPTER 8

Stocks That Soar Over Time: Marathon Stocks for Late Starters

How to Choose High-Growth Stocks

"In the wide Sargasso Sea of middle age, two things loom ahead: the rest of your life and living in comfort."

Evonne Hurst quietly commands a large Holiday Inn ballroom in Madison, Wisconsin, with the confidence of someone who has organized stock investment fairs over the past two decades. She started doing this during a time when stocks were about as popular as root canal operations, and became one of the leaders of a movement largely consisting of middle-class women. Starting with $10 a month, she has built a portfolio that translates into a comfortable income and the ability to expand one of her hobbies—organizing more investment club fairs. As a founding mother of the famed Milwaukee investment club fair in the mid-1970s, she's well versed in what individual investors want from a stock.

Although she's an accountant with her own business, she was never formally trained to analyze stocks, is not a Wall Street insider, and keeps company with those who are like-minded in that they prefer to invest in Wisconsin-based companies that rarely make the front page of *The Wall Street Journal.*

Evonne gazes over her glasses with a warm "trust me" look as I sit at an investment club regional congress organized by her and the volunteers of the newly formed Southwest Wisconsin Council of the National Association of Investors Corporation (NAIC), the 750,000-member, nonprofit group that is the guiding yet very visible hand behind organized investment clubs in the United States.

"Investment clubs are great equalizers," Hurst says of the diverse mix of members. "There is no caste system and it doesn't matter who you are or how much money you make." Evonne has assembled the deans of investment clubbing for this event. Kenneth Janke, Sr., the chief executive officer of the NAIC, has squeezed a keynote in between his playing in an NFL celebrity golf tournament. Also on the dais is Tom O'Hara, the venerable chairman of the NAIC and one of the founding members of the NAIC, who is also a member of the seminal Mutual Investment Club of Detroit, which just passed the $4 million mark in assets after fifty-seven years of operations by ordinary guys. Tom's son, Bob, is one of the managers of the NAIC's growing operations in Madison Heights, Michigan, a suburb of Detroit. Peggy Schmeltz, another ace NAIC organizer and a member of the board of trustees, has chosen to attend the fair in lieu of her husband Bill's reunion at Harvard. Like the others, she has achieved a remarkable level of success investing in stocks as a member of the First Ladies Club (and others) and has spent decades passing it along to others with no background in investing.

Janke is concerned that most investors today are unprepared for a market downturn. Less than half of NAIC members—many of whom are baby boomers saving for retirement—have seen a bear market, Janke notes. He's aware that market dips may sway investors from concentrating on long-term results, and that the inevitable market trough might turn away those that need to invest the most.

Janke observes that since the turn of the century, a market correction of 10% or more has occurred every two years, an event that hasn't happened since 1990, but that may have changed as you read this. In the dismal 1973–74 bear market, when the economy was racked by high inflation that was triple what it is today, stocks turned down some 48%. Janke and the oldest investment club members weathered that storm and have enjoyed the fruits of investing in stocks when others retreated to money market funds, CDs, and real estate. The silver lining of Janke's outlook is that for every bear market, the market goes up *three times* as much. So if you pick a handful of solid, dividend/earnings producing stocks, it's possible to double your money in five years.

The proven profitability of Janke's (and the NAIC's) strategy speaks for itself. If you contributed just $2,000 a year into an IRA of growth stocks over twenty years at 12% (your principal doubles every six years), you'd have $1.9 million at the end of the period, assuming dividends and gains are left in the kitty to compound.

Although Janke's club is all men, 60% of the NAIC is composed of women. Few are educated directly in the ways of Wall Street. There are grandmothers, housewives, secretaries, and executives in clubs. Men, of course, are members, but do best when combined with women. Over time, all-women clubs outperform the all-men clubs, but the mixed-gender clubs do best overall.

The overwhelming success of investment clubs is due to the fact that they can and do beat the market on a regular basis with long-term stock investing principles. Even if you have less than fifteen years to go before you say good-bye to the conventional workplace, an investment club is a workable and social setting for you to learn quickly about investing. The ground rules for finding a few "marathon" stocks that will outrun inflation, the general market, and business cycles are deceptively simple and take only a few weeks to learn.

Principles of Marathon Stock Investing

As a golfer, Ken Janke loves to hit the course wherever he travels. While investor education keeps him on the road for a great deal of the year, at-home education finds a place on his bookshelf. He has an extensive collection of books on golf. During the cold winter months of the upper Midwest, Janke knows he can retreat to his

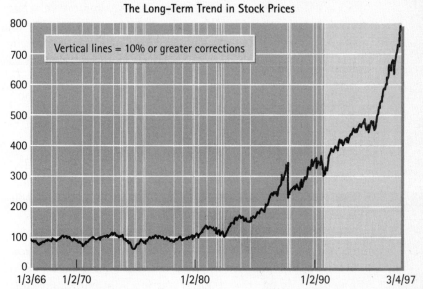

INVESTING LONG-TERM IN STOCKS: A WINNING STRATEGY
The Long-Term Trend in Stock Prices

Vertical lines = 10% or greater corrections

Daily Data 1/3/66–3/4/97
SOURCE: T. Rowe Price Associates

den and at least read about his favorite sport. Janke exemplifies a model of prosperity that is one of the enduring qualities of marathon stock investors. He keeps on reading, researching, and picking companies that are good investment values. Through his club and personal portfolio, though, he needn't plunge wholeheartedly into one stock at one time. His horizon extends at least five years and can span several decades if the company's management keeps on producing satisfactory numbers. Investment clubbers typically start out small, usually putting in $25 a month and pooling their money with others to buy stocks at good prices. The following are the keys to their success:

- **Invest regularly.** Whether it's $25 a month or $100 a month, keep your money flowing into your investments during all market conditions. By employing dollar-cost averaging, you avoid buying in at the absolute highs or lows. According to a University of Michigan study, some 95% of market gains came in at just 1.2% of a given year's trading days, so there's no point in trying to guess when the market's highs and lows are going to occur.

- **Reinvest dividends.** Putting the money you earn right back into new shares adds to the power of compounding your dollars invested. In dividend reinvestment plans, dividends are invested in new shares, which means you also are buying those new shares at no commission. So the automatic compounding comes at no extra cost to you. Dividend reinvesting also adds to your total return (capital gains plus income reinvested).

- **Find better-than-average companies.** You might think this is the most difficult part of your investment strategy, but it's also relatively simple. A company with sales and earnings per share growth of 15% will double in value every five years or so. A number of sources will identify these companies for you (see *Value Line* or the Resources section). If you do a little more homework, you can buy these companies at a good price relative to other stocks and the market.

"It makes no difference when you begin, commitment is the key," Janke emphasizes. "Even if you invested $2,000 a year in the Standard & Poor's 500 index at the worst possible times during market peaks over the past twenty years, your $40,000 stake would be worth $171,757 after the two decades," he adds, citing a T. Rowe Price study.

An Enlightened View of Risk: A Case Study

About five years ago, my wife Kathleen decided she wanted to take her mare, Tara, out for a ride out behind our house, which is a 1,000-acre-plus farm. As the sky grew dark, I became concerned, because the wind was picking up and I could see a thunderstorm was approaching from the southwest. Since Kathleen's an experienced and smart rider, I'd knew she'd be in soon. She also had one of our German shepherds, Ella, with her, so I knew if Kathleen had any problems about riding in a storm, Ella would get her back home. Well, minutes turned into hours as I watched the horizon for my wife and Ella to appear. The wind started to howl. The big oaks near our barn heaved. When the storm was just about on top of us, Kathleen, Tara, and Ella pulled up to the side of the barn. I was relieved, and I ran out to help Kathleen dismount just as it started to pour. As I went to grab Tara's bridle so that Kathleen could dismount, a blinding flash of lightning hit an oak no more than five feet behind us. The tremendous boom instantly told me that the oak had acted as a lightning rod.

My next thought was that Tara was going to bolt. Fortunately, Kathleen had jumped before the mare made her move. To our surprise, though, Tara did a quarter turn and held her ground. This was atypical of a thoroughbred mare. Most horses would've been in the next county under those circumstances. Most thoroughbreds would've hightailed it back to Kentucky. We were lucky. Tara snorted. Ella rubbed her ears. I looked at the oak. The electrical bolt had blown a three-inch sheath from the tree's bark that landed thirty feet away.

Now you're probably wondering what this horse story has to do with the stock market. Your most prized growth stocks are the thoroughbreds of the market. Now imagine that the market is this thunderstorm waiting to hurl thunderbolts at your portfolio and spook your stocks. When a market can drop from 170 to 500 points in a day, and nervous institutions are ready to jump out of the storm at any second with the aid of lightning-quick computers, what's an individual investor to do? Wear a *HAT* to keep you dry. This is an acronym that will help you diversify, reduce risk, and find growth outside of mutual funds.

The Simple HAT Approach to Picking Marathon Stocks

By donning a HAT, I'm not referring to a *chapeau,* a bowler, or a fez. HAT is my acronym for *health/home, aging,* and *technology.* These four stock-investing themes will propel any late-start investor into an age of New Prosperity and insulate you from the turbulence of business cycles and unsteady markets. These sectors, represented by specific companies, will also lend some purpose to your stock investing.

Home and health are at the core of this strategy and are interlinked. Any product that is relatively inexpensive and can be used in any home around the world may also be used by people to enhance their health. Products like consumer goods—everything from disposable shavers (Gillette) to drugs (Merck, Johnson & Johnson)—fit this bill. These are relatively recession-proof companies. Consumers will not cut back on lifesaving drugs or on soap and toothpaste, such as those produced by Colgate-Palmolive, during an economic downturn, so they are not impacted by business cycles. Of course you needn't pick these stocks exclusively. Any profitable, well-managed stocks bought at a reasonable price will fit the bill for a prudent investment.

It's also fairly well documented that the world's mature industrial nations are, well, maturing. Demographically, large segments of the population in the United States, Germany, Japan, France, and the United Kingdom are growing older. This aging of large populations translates into greater demand for companies such as United Healthcare.

Remember how many prescriptions you needed when you were 21? Compare that number with the variety of prescriptions you have now or the bottles in your parents' medicine cabinets. Modern pharmaceuticals are not only lifesavers, they reduce—or make unnecessary—the need for some surgeries, help cure previously incurable diseases (like cancer and heart disease), and reduce the overall cost of health care. All of that could translate into a big plus for your portfolio for the next twenty years or so if you want to invest in stocks that produce these things.

The Brim of the HAT: Technology

Modern industrial society is also riding on technology, telecommunications, and software, the newest, fastest steeds of capitalism. These horses are still in the starting gate. Today the market leaders rule over a world that largely doesn't even exist in the traditional tangible sense—computing and cyberspace.

How fast is the technology market moving? At the speed of light. Consider this:

- Personal computer sales now exceed those of televisions (in U.S. unit sales); more than 60 million PCs were sold in the United States in 1996, according to the Electronic Industries Association, a trade group.

- U.S. companies maintain global market-share leads of 60% to 90% in key technology industries. PC companies alone account for a quarter *trillion* dollars of market capitalization.

- Every two *seconds*, a personal computer with an Intel microprocessor is sold.

- Countries with emerging economies such as China and its neighbors in the Far East are asking American-based companies to invest in cellular telephones and other high-tech amenities.

- Electronic mail has galloped past the U.S. Postal Service in number of message units sent. For most progressive companies, technology *is* productivity and improved profits.

What does all of this mean? To shrewd investors, nearly any mutual fund or individual investor who bought microprocessor, software, or Internet technologies issues could have easily doubled their money over the last eighteen months. This doesn't happen too often in the history of the stock market.

Technology is an odd duck that waddles through just about every business, and if you've ever experienced technical problems, you'll agree that *waddle* is the correct verb here. The nature of technology is that despite its shortcomings it enhances productivity for every business on every level, especially when it comes to software (Microsoft), processing (Intel), financial services (GE), and telecommunications (Motorola).

A Brief Word on Timing the Market:
An Example of Why You Hold Stocks

If you have the time to pick stocks and adopt my HAT strategy, there's a good chance that you'll pick a handful of great stocks and see institutions (mutual funds, pension funds, insurers) beat down the price as if these companies weren't going to make another cent in earnings. Well, remember that time—not timing—is on your side. Here's a compelling figure: Between 1926 and 1993, 99% of the market's gains occurred in just forty-eight months. That means if you kept $100 in the market that entire time it would return $63,760. Now, if you timed the market and missed only twelve of those forty-eight months, you would've only made $6,500. So by basically staying put, you have the potential to increase your returns by a factor of ten.

But the market's volatile, you say. Even good stocks look bad when Wall Street's in a bad mood. Remember, just stay put and you'll be okay if you've done your homework. Here's an example: One of my favorite examples of a good stay-put stock is Motorola. As you know, Motorola makes cell phones, chips, and pagers and is very good at what it does. Unfortunately, or fortunately for most of us, Motorola is one of the top holdings of institutions. As such, every time the institutions want to sell, they dump Motorola.

During 1996, for example, through no fault of its own, Motorola was priced as low as $47 and as high as $80. Now, you ask, how can a company generally regarded as an earnings machine and innovator lose nearly half of its market cap in such as short span of time? One reason—and one that I urge you to pay no attention to—is that institutions sell on one piece of news that ignores the rest of the company's picture. In Motorola's case, it is the growing prospect that the cell-phone market in the United States is slowing down and becoming less profitable. For one thing, Motorola has a lot of competition. Nokia, Ericsson, and a whole host of Japanese companies produce the same products. That puts what Wall Street calls pricing pressures on the company. Competitors sell their products for less. That means Motorola has to cut its prices. That means lower profits, right? Yes, you must remember that these events happen in cycles. You buy when the cycle "shakes out" and the company's earnings are down. When the institutions are selling, you can be buying. If the company still looks good, you will be buying it at a great price. You can also dollar-cost average. You can apply this strategy to *all* of the companies in your portfolio. Keep in mind that you have to look at these things holistically.

As this goes to press, Motorola was taking its lumps, however. Worldwide demand slackened for its cellular telephones, its Asian customers were nailed by widespread economic downturns, and its global competition was eating its lunch through pricing wars. The company was also late to the game in marketing digital cell phones and its chip-making business was sagging. As a result, the company's stock price dipped into the fifties (from the eighties a year ago), and management said it was studying restructuring.

As a late-start investor, what would you do with a company like this? If you have less than five years to invest, I'd say sell it. But long-term research shows that this is the kind of company you want to keep for the long haul. The future still looks good for nearly every Motorola business. The management is still competent, it's still firmly entrenched in growth markets across the world, and its lower price makes it a better buy—especially if you dollar-cost average through a dividend reinvestment plan. Remember, one of the keys to being a successful late-start investor is patience and staying focused on your long-term goals. If a company (or companies or mutual funds) offer you growth over the long term, hold on to them and buy them when the market gives you a better buying opportunity. If you've done your research, stay the course. The market will reward you for your courage.

Keeping Up With Research

Wall Street is generally a coward when it comes to bad news. It stumbles away from a housecat, thinking it's a tiger. The key is research. If you have the time, here's what you need to do.

First, if you do nothing during your monitoring of companies, keep a clippings file. Look up stories on the company in the library's *Business Index* CD-ROM. This service is your best friend.

Print out the stories. Do they indicate a company's fortunes are changing for the worse? Are earnings dropping substantially? If so, are they short-term events or signals that the company is in for a long downturn?

Then scan publications like *Business Week, The Wall Street Journal, Barron's,* and your pick of the best value-oriented newsletters. Copy those articles on companies that interest you and ask the same questions you've already asked. Both the *Journal* and *Barron's* have convenient company indexes that will give you page numbers of any articles referring to companies you are following. That way, you don't have to read the papers all the way through to find what you need.

Other great resources are either America Online, CompuServe, or the Internet. All have excellent research sections that allow you to monitor every press release and report on a company. You can even access the Internet to get a hold of SEC reports online at www.sec.gov. Look at 10-K and 10-Q reports for no-nonsense appraisals of where the companies see problems. These are the annual and quarterly reports that the companies must file with the SEC, so they have to be somewhat honest.

Let's go back to Motorola for a moment. We all try to look for ideal companies. These are companies that seemingly outlast recessions, interest-rate spikes, and government intervention; have great international exposure; and grow at least 14.4% a year. Where does the company see its growth coming from? Through my research, I discovered that Motorola is attempting to become a major player in bringing the Internet into every home. They are making things called cable modems that turn cable TV into an access route to the Internet. That's a huge source of potential profit. Other profit centers are in Motorola's investments in Asia, where they have plants and dominant market share in producing and selling cell phones and pagers. Since China and India have a lot of people with relatively few communications devices, this is another avenue for future profits.

As I continue to research, I find out the bad news. Although Motorola is growing at 14% a year to more than $30 billion in annual sales, it's under pressure to become a consumer company, which it is really isn't. Motorola is playing second fiddle to Intel in the chip-making business. And chip prices, due to the nature of the market for chips, fall in price by 50% when they become commodities. And if you read Motorola's reports filed with the SEC, which are available on the Internet through the EDGAR service, you see they've got environmental problems at some of their Arizona chip-making plants. Even the great British magazine *The Economist* says Motorola's facing an uphill battle when it comes to the brave new world of technology marketing. So do you listen to the institutions and sell? Or not?

Well, let's return to our research to see if there's a nasty storm coming. Check the company's SEC filings. Skip the annual report. Let's see what they tell the government, where they sort of tell the truth. Well, they're honest about a big IRS audit, a wrongful death suit, and their competitive and pollution problems. But in the words of Wall Street, none of these omens will have an "adverse material impact." That means that if their earnings continue to rise the way they have been, we're okay. I'm going to hold on to this stock despite the Asian economic crisis in 1997 and problems that may lie ahead. I'm looking twenty years down the road. I recommend that you take this long-term view with the stocks you own as well.

The Bottom Line:
What You Absolutely Need to Know About a Stock

Questions you must ask are:

1. Is the company continuing to boost earnings?

2. Is it piling up debt for capital investment or acquisitions that don't build the bottom line?

3. If it's experiencing earnings slumps, are they temporary or long-term?

Performance Bonus: Buy Stocks After They Split

Another good sign for a company is a consistent record of stock splits. I know Warren Buffett doesn't believe in them, but companies that split consistently beat the market. Remember stock prices are powered by earnings. If the earnings aren't there, investors won't be attracted to the company and there's no capital appreciation. Splits keep investors interested and present great times to buy. A Rice University study has shown that 1,275 companies that split 2-for-1 from 1975 to 1990 outperformed companies of similar size that had no stock splits. The margin of outperformance between these two groups ranged from 8% to 12%. To quote the study, "most managers of companies with relatively high-priced stocks choose to split them only if they are fairly confident that the new share prices will not fall too far. . . . So they tend to act when corporate prospects are favorable."

Finally: What Are Some Marathon Companies?

What's a marathon company in a nutshell? Again, they are companies that consistently put up earnings increases, gain market share, increase their international exposure, and innovate like crazy. The following companies fit that bill:

Stock	Business	Dividend Reinvestment Plan
AFLAC	Insurance	Y
Coca-Cola	Soft drinks	Y
Colgate-Palmolive	Consumer goods	Y
GE	Financial, industrial	Y
Gillette	Consumer goods	N
Intel	Semiconductors	N
Johnson & Johnson	Drugs, health care	Y
McDonald's	Food	Y
Microsoft	Software	N
RPM	Paints, coatings	Y

Stock	Business	Dividend Reinvestment Plan
Merck	Pharmaceuticals	Y
Motorola	Cell phones, telecom	Y
United Healthcare	Managed care	N

NOTE: Companies with dividend reinvestment plans allow you to invest in new shares automatically without paying a commission through a broker. You need only one share to enroll. Contact the individual companies' investor relations departments for more details.

COMPANIES WITH LARGE OVERSEAS SALES

These companies can give you international exposure and more diversification.

Company	Foreign Sales	
	% Total Sales	**% of Profits**
Coca-Cola	68	79
Colgate-Palmolive	68	68
Gillette	68	70
McDonald's	50	50
Johnson & Johnson	50	48
Merck	30	29

Source: Annual reports (1996)

Summary: Stocks, Brokers, and Common Sense

Pay as little as you can to buy stocks. Although brokers will try to offer you their hot picks or research, this information is tainted.

Brokers are compensated for selling products, not according to whether you make money or not. Since everything brokers sell generates a commission, they actually make more money if their picks don't work out because they make money when you buy and sell. Trust your instincts and the quality of your research. In my experience, too many people insist on using a broker's advice. Sure, there are great brokers with great tips, but you have to keep in mind that they are compensated no matter how much you *lose* money. If they pick bombs for you, they make money. If their pick has a big run-up and you sell, they make money again. When you buy the next best thing, there's another commission. Brokers are salespeople, first and foremost. Just keep that in mind. Here are a few ways to keep from getting fleeced:

- **When it comes to new ideas for stocks, the best place to look is in your supermarket, your shopping mall, your office, your doctor's office, your hardware store, and especially your library.** There are hundreds of ideas within the pages of *Value Line*, *Standard & Poor's*, *Business Week*, *Forbes*, *Barron's*, and *The Wall Street Journal*. The best ideas are usually your own. The neat thing about these resources are that they're all in the library for free.

- **If you do pick a broker, pick one that's just going to make transactions for you at the lowest possible cost.** I came across a useful survey recently for the magazine on full-service brokers. The National Council of Individual Investors found that brokerage commissions varied up to 638% from the highest to the lowest— and that's just among full-service brokers. NCII did a survey of the top full-service and bank-affiliated brokers and rated them for commissions, fees, investment analysis, and disciplinary history. In other words, they were looking for the cheapest, most honest brokers among the big boys.

- **Can you imagine paying a broker a fee to reinvest your dividends or for postage and handling?** I love to find companies that charge fees like this to point out to my readers who to avoid. But brokers will get you for these fees, so you have to watch out. Another little-known tip about brokers is that their commissions are negotiable. If you're doing business with a full-service broker, ask him if he will meet the commission from the best discount broker. If he values your account—and you threaten to take it elsewhere—he will usually meet you at least halfway, if not all the way. Full service at discount prices. Why not? This business is so competitive that brokers will do anything to get your account; it's up to you to see what they'll do to keep it. Check out the ads in *The Wall Street Journal* or *Barron's*.

- **Now if you just want to get a broker to fill your orders, which is the way I like my brokers, go "cheap and deep."** Deep-discounters will go as low as $7 a trade. Check out the ads in *Barron's* for the most current deals. There's a huge shakeout going on in this business. The winners will do whatever it takes to serve you, the investor. The big boys can't take all the marbles; there are plenty of scrappy players. There are always brokerage houses with deep-discount rates eager for your business. To save even more money, you can trade yourself through the Internet. Just plug "discount brokers" into any search engine (like www.infoseek.com or www.yahoo.com) and you'll find dozens of online trading sites.

- **You don't need to buy government bonds through brokers.** You can buy them directly from the government through the Bureau of Public Debt or Federal Reserve Bank branches. Check your white pages for listings of branches near you.

- **Don't buy mutual funds through brokers.** You can buy no-load, low-expense funds directly through fund companies. Not only do brokers have nothing to do with the management of the funds they sell you, you pay a commission for little or no advice and your assets are nicked to market the funds to others.

- **If you buy a stock through a broker, you don't have to keep it with them.** Most brokers will want to keep your stock in a "street name," meaning you don't get a certificate or belong to the company's dividend reinvestment plan (DRIP). This encourages you to buy and sell through that broker, naturally "earning" him commissions when you do. You can always obtain the certificates and sell them through the lowest-commission broker you can find. Or you could buy one share and enroll in the company's DRIP. This is an even better deal for you.

- **Avoid brokers entirely by buying directly from the company.** Although only a handful of companies offer this option, you pay no commission when you buy direct from the company.

- **Invest directly in companies through DRIPs and never pay another commission.** When you buy one share, you enroll yourself in the DRIP—if the company has one. Then all subsequent dividends and new shares are purchased commission-free. This is a great tool for regular investing.

- **Don't buy special issue bonds or initial public offerings from brokers.** Chances are very good that you are not getting a good price on these issues, since the best deals are reserved for the biggest customers. These securities also tend to be extremely volatile. They may move 100% in one day. Even if you have "inside information" on the next hot/best thing, stay away from these come-ons.

- **Don't buy commodities through brokers.** Although you're starting late, commodities are among the riskiest investments you can buy. You can lose more than you invested in margin accounts that employ generous credit to buy more securities.

- **Don't buy certificates of deposit (CDs) through brokers.** You can do better shopping for yourself. The single best source on this is the *Bank Rate Monitor/100 Highest Yields* newsletter, which lists the top-yielding CDs nationwide. The service is free if you have access to the Internet (www.bankrate.com).

- **Avoid broker "wrap" accounts.** These are money-management vehicles that feature in-house money managers. These accounts are loaded with fees and the managers usually underperform a common stock-index mutual fund. You're better off managing your own money. Not only do you have more control, it'll cost you less, so you'll have more to invest.

- **Don't confuse investment consultants with investment advisers.** Securities brokers call themselves consultants, but they don't really consult anybody on the best possible investment advice for you. They're in it for the commissions. You can hire an investment adviser, but make sure he or she is registered with the SEC and review his or her form ADV, which any adviser must show you if he or she is a true registered investment adviser. This form will disclose any possible conflicts of interest. If you need yet another level of financial planning expertise, consult a certified financial planner, who is required to have at least two years of education in addition to basic financial expertise.

- **Obtain free investment research on the Internet.** It's amazing how much is available there now. Brokers lure clients in by offering them free "research," which features only the stocks the brokerage house wants to sell you. Speaking of the Internet, don't buy just any stock promoted there. Cyberspace is full of sharks, so check out the Resources section at the end of this book for the best Internet sites.

CHAPTER 9

Anchoring Your Portfolio: The Role of Bonds

How Income Can Serve You Best

"Life and bonds are both debts; bonds pay interest, but only life can pay dividends."

Tom Geoghegan is a lawyer/author friend of mine who is hard-working and intelligent and has a good heart. Unfortunately, at 50, he's just starting to invest for his New Prosperity, although he has a 401(k) that's doing nicely. He would like to write, produce a play, travel, and pursue public-interest law. Where are most of his non-401(k) retirement savings? In a savings account. After I read him the riot act about how his money is losing money due to the ravages of inflation, I asked him what he wanted to do with his money and when he wanted to do it. Not surprisingly, like a lot of us, he wanted to do something completely different in the near future and wanted the money to enable him to make his vocational change. His first instinct was to invest in bonds, which are the fallback position for safety in any investment portfolio, although they offer little to no growth of capital. While bonds have their place in most late-start portfolios, they should never be the dominant vehicle in any portfolio, I told him. I'm not sure if he took my advice to heart, so I suggested he concentrate on growth mutual funds instead.

Bonds are pretty simple animals. They're the tortoises of invest-ments. They move pretty slowly, but they eventually get to their destination while paying steady dividends in the form of interest. If you need to preserve capital and reap income over an extended pe-riod of time, you buy bonds. Unless you choose really badly—and that's hard to do in the bond world—the bonds will be there for you. Since bonds are great at storing capital and providing an in-come stream, they're best used in retirement or within four years or more of retirement. That applies if you are taking a conventional retirement at age 65 or 67. If you have more time, you need growth, growth, and more growth.

Bonds have a place in anyone's portfolio, but are often misun-derstood. Bonds are generally thought of as "safe" investments. That means unless the bond issuer defaults and suddenly refuses to pay interest, you'll get your regular income payments. Bonds are not safe, however, when it comes to beating inflation, because bond payments or "coupons" are fixed when you buy them. One excep-tion is the new breed of inflation-indexed Treasury securities, but more on that later. Keep in mind that no *income* investment can truly outpace the total return from stocks, which as a group have consistently beaten inflation. As you know, at the current con-sumer price index inflation rate, today's dollar is worth about 4% less next year; in eighteen years that dollar will be worth 50¢. In-come investments before retirement, however, have a very well de-fined place in your portfolio. Use them wisely, but be realistic about what they can do for you.

As there is an art to picking stocks and stock mutual funds, you have to be just as careful in picking income vehicles. Few people re-alize that in the noninflationary, nonrecessionary year of 1994 that thirty-year U.S. Treasury bonds lost 30% of their market value (if you bought them at the beginning of the year and sold them De-cember 31). Of course, that was a year in which the Federal Reserve raised interest rates. If you held on to your bonds, preferably until maturity, you didn't lose anything. Most income investors don't actively trade their bonds, but if you need income at a certain date for some reason and have to sell your bonds, you could get caught short if you sell them before maturity.[1]

Bond Basics: What Makes Them Go Up and Down

Bonds are instruments of credit: they represent a promise to pay back a debt. When you buy a bond, you are loaning the issuer money. In return, you are paid back the principal with interest over time. Savings bonds, Treasury bills, notes and bonds, corporate bonds, mortgage bonds, and other instruments tied into promises of repayment are all *debt equities*. Their value is determined by

1. the financial stability of the lender or credit risk (or political stability if the bond is underwritten by a government)

2. current interest rates for that maturity

3. what investors are willing to pay for that bond based on what their money can do in other markets.

Interest rates move bond prices—the value of principal in the open market—because yields are based on prevailing rates. The lower the risk, the lower the rate. The same applies to maturities. If you are willing to hold a bond for twenty or thirty years, you get a premium rate. If you are willing to hold a bond for only ninety days, you're getting a short-term money market rate that's pretty close to the rate of inflation at the time.

Rising interest rates push bond prices down. In an open market, that means investors holding lower-yielding vehicles will want to get those higher yields. Since yields are fixed on nearly all income instruments, the lower-yielding bonds will have less relative value. The smarter money is always chasing the better returns. When rates are dropping in the overall market, investors find that the older securities—with higher yields—are more valuable to them, so the prices of those vehicles rises.

Yields are also higher on bonds rated as higher credit risks—for example, high-yield junk corporate bonds. If a recession or other setback impairs a company's ability to pay bondholders, then those investors might be left holding the bag—hence the "risk premium" in the form of higher yields. Mortgage-backed bonds such as Ginnie Maes are backed with home mortgages, but tend to be much more secure instruments.

There is a wide universe of bonds categorized according to the issuer and their maturity. The lowest-yielding, most secure vehicles are either U.S. Treasury bills or corporate paper with maturity periods under one year. You climb the yield ladder from there, going to bonds with maturities up to forty years. The following is a sample of the wide world of bonds, all of which are packaged in thousands of different mutual funds.

A PRIMER ON BONDS

Issuer	Maturity/type	Relative Yield	Safety*
U.S. government	90-day/1 yr T-bills	low	highest
Money market	90-day/corp.	low	high
U.S. government	2–10 yr T-notes	moderate	solid
High-quality corp.	2–10 yr corp. bonds	moderate	good
U.S. agencies	5 yrs+ mortgages	higher	good
U.S. government	30-yr T-bonds	highest	volatile
Corporate	High-yield (junk)	highest	risky
Muncipal	All maturities	varies	moderate

* Safety refers to credit risk or the chance the bond issuer will default on your income payments. All bonds, except for those held to maturity and short-term instruments, are subject to market risk when interest rates rise and fall.

How to Use Income Investments

There are three reasons why you should put a small portion of your money into income investments: diversification, cash management, and current income needs. The diversification need is simple: Bonds provide a buffer against stock-market declines (see the chart on page 184). Although sometimes bonds precede stocks in downturns, in most cases they move inversely to stocks during dips. Since your salary or other employment income is providing for current income, you needn't worry about that component of your financial plan until you retire. Cash management and diversification are essential, although they are poorly understood.

Cash Management. Cash management makes all of your free cash work for you. This is a simple concept that eludes most people who just want to balance their checkbooks. Other than the money you carry in your wallet, it makes sense for you to put every dollar to work when it isn't going out the door to pay bills to work for you. Typically this means that any money not immediately needed in checking or short-term savings can be earning the highest possible yields. Choose the highest-yielding money market mutual funds with the lowest possible fees. Check *The Wall Street Journal, Barron's Money*, or www.ibcdata.com on the Internet for the best money market rates nationwide.

Escrow Account Funds. This is the fund your mortgage company requires you hold up to a year's worth of taxes and often insurance payments in. You may have thousands sitting in here not earning a dime. Either ask your bank to pay a market rate of interest on such an account—equal to the rate on ninety-day U.S. Treasury bills—or close the account. The bank's earning money on your idle cash, so why shouldn't you? If you choose to open your own escrow account, you can choose a high-yielding money market fund (see the following page) and automatically withdraw the funds from your checking account to fund it. You simply write the check when your property taxes come due.

Special Savings. Almost nobody puts aside money into *checking* for special events such as holidays, birthdays, weddings, or special purchases such as home down payments, cars, or boats. Under an efficient cash-management plan, you should establish a special savings fund to put money aside at the safest, highest yields you can find.

Emergency Funds. While financial planners recommend you keep up to six months worth of take-home pay in an emergency fund, it's rare to find anyone who does. Everyone needs one, however. Those with seasonal employment or in a volatile job situation definitely need to do this. You also never know when a huge bill for the dentist, your mechanic, or a new hot water heater will pop up.

Sources for cash-management accounts include money market mutual funds, U.S. Treasury money market funds, and short-term corporate bond funds. If you are adventurous and are willing to accept more risk for greater return, you can use a high-quality corporate bond fund, a Ginnie Mae fund, or a high-yield (junk) bond fund for your idle cash. These funds, of course, can lose principal if the bond market turns south. The safest funds are your government-only money market funds. Certificates of deposit may be a good idea if you know exactly when you will need the money and can afford to lock it up for a year or so. Avoid, however, gimmick CDs tied into the stock market. If you want to invest in the stock market, that's another game entirely and you should invest in it directly through stocks or indirectly through no-load stock mutual funds.

Use Income Investments to Buffer Your Stock Positions

Conventional wisdom once held that bonds always move in the opposite direction of stocks. That's no longer true all of the time. Huge retreats in the bond markets often force sell-offs in stocks because large money managers such as banks, insurance firms, and pension funds must make up the difference from their bond losses by taking gains in stocks. So the idea that merely holding bonds

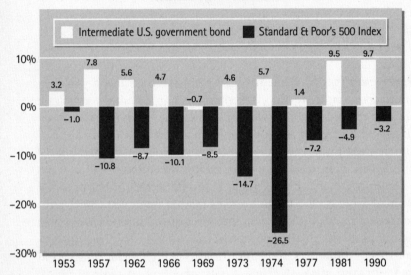

BONDS CAN INSULATE YOUR PORTFOLIO
Calendar Year Total Returns

Intermediate U.S. government bond   Standard & Poor's 500 Index

The bars show performance of stocks in every calendar year since 1950 in which they produced a negative return and the corresponding return on bonds in the same years.

SOURCE: T. Rowe Price Associates

will protect you from the roller-coaster stock market creates a false sense of security. Nevertheless, if you hold your bonds to maturity or have short-term vehicles like money market funds, you really have little to worry about.

The key to finding stability in your bond portfolio lies in what type of bonds and bond funds you hold. As we noted above, the shorter the maturity and the higher the credit "quality" of a bond, the less volatility you'll find. If you are buying a bond mutual fund, check its *duration*. This is a key measure of risk that tells you what happens to bonds in the portfolio if interest rates rise 1%. A higher duration means a higher risk. For example, if duration is 10 and rates rise ½ of 1%, then your fund will decline 5%. Of course, the closer you are to retirement, the more your portfolio should be buffered with high-quality bonds and bond funds. But don't limit your income-investment diversification to bonds.

Not All Income Investments Are Bonds

This is a versatile arena of income investing that gives late-start investors a particular advantage. Convertible bonds and high-yield stocks—whether in the form of dividends or preferred shares— offer the promise of relatively high yields and the upside potential of capital gains. Convertible bonds are hybrid securities that can be converted into stocks at a future date. High-yield/preferred stocks are usually those of older companies that want investors to keep their shares and entice them to do so by offering them dividends in the range of 2% to 5%. Utilities and pharmaceutical companies typically offer high dividends. Both industries are prone to the excesses of the market, however. Over the next few years, deregulation will force some radical restructuring within the utilities industry. Drug stocks were pummeled in 1992–93 when a national-health plan was proposed by the Clinton administration. That time offered some phenomenal bargains in some of the most solid names in the business, all of which carried high yields. Above-average dividends give you a little insulation during market tempests. Investors are less likely to dump stocks with healthy dividends than companies that don't pay out as much.

Dividends represent a portion of the company's profit passed along to investors. Companies without solid profit streams tend to be much more volatile in market down-turns. Dividends provide an extra layer of insulation; that's essential for late-start investing.

Buying U.S. Treasuries

A natural question at this point is: if U.S. government securities are among the safest investments to buy, why shouldn't they dominate a late-start portfolio? After all,

LATE-STARTER TIP

The closer you are to retirement, the more you should diversify your portfolio with income investments. If you are less than ten years away, consider having from 40% to 60% of your portfolio in bonds or money market funds.

isn't it too late in the game to be taking big risks? Remember that Treasury securities—when held to maturity—pose no real credit risk (barring a massive collapse of the U.S. Treasury), since the notes are backed by the "full faith and credit" of the U.S. government. Although you are buying Washington's debts when you purchase a Treasury bond, Congress can always raise taxes to back up its paper. Yes, Treasury securities will provide modest insulation to your portfolio. No, they won't provide any growth. That's why the safe approach will not only fail to beat inflation, it will fail to build up your portfolio in a relatively short period of time.

Having a few T-bonds or notes in your portfolio provides you with a solid, fail-safe position. You know the money will be there from ten to thirty years from now. It doesn't make much sense, however, to buy T-bills or "pass-through" government-guaranteed mortgages. They usually come in large denominations ($10,000 or more) and are better incorporated into bond mutual funds. T-bills are usually the mainstay of Treasury-only or "general purpose" money market funds. If you want to anchor your late-start portfolio, no more than one-fifth of it should be comprised of T-bonds or notes.

The cheapest way to buy Treasury securities is to buy them directly from the government. Through its Treasury Direct program, the U.S. Treasury will automatically deposit interest electronically into an account of your choice for any bonds you purchase. Bonds and notes are sold at regular "auctions." When you buy them, you are essentially submitting a "noncompetitive bid."

The other way of buying T-bonds is through any stockbroker. They will, of course, charge you a commission—unless you can negotiate that out of the sale. Any commission naturally reduces your total return of what you're buying, so it's not in your best interest to use a broker and pay an unnecessary commission. If you have an ongoing relationship with a broker, however, he might cut the commission as a cost of doing future business. Ask him. Smart brokers will gladly forgo a small commission for the prospect of a profitable relationship.

If you feel safer with a larger percentage of Treasury bonds in your portfolio, stagger the maturities, or ladder them. This will reduce

your overall interest-rate risk. A sample T-bond portfolio might con-
sist of five-, ten-, twenty- and thirty-year bonds. That way, if interest rates rise, you won't be too far behind in getting the best yields.

The Treasury also offers inflation-indexed bonds, which will make
up the difference in the loss of principal based on the consumer price
index. For what you don't get in yield, you can do much better in
other income investments. They're a good deal as far as bonds go, because most don't index to inflation. Keep in mind, however, that if
you really want to beat inflation—and not keep pace with it—you
need to invest in growth vehicles. That means stocks.

Within your income portfolio, you will need to ladder the maturities of the T-bonds you buy to reduce risk. As we discussed, the
longer the maturity, the greater the market risk and the higher the
yield. Laddering buffers the risk and offers you some diversity.
Here's an example:

LADDERED TREASURY PORTFOLIO

Maturity	Yield (percent)
3 mos.	5.08
6 mos.	5.42
1 year	5.83
2 years	6.24
3 years	6.37
5 years	6.53
10 years	6.66

NOTE: All yields subject to change. This is for demonstration purposes only.

See how the interest rate rises with the maturity? Your average
yield will be lower if you ladder out your bonds, but your overall
risk will be lower. You can, of course, buy zero-coupon treasuries

LATE-STARTER TIP

Buying U.S. Treasury Bonds and Notes. You can contact any Federal Reserve branch bank (check the government listings of your phone book). Also call 214-922-6100 or check out the Internet at www.frbsf.org. A central source of information is the Bureau of Public Debt at 202-874-4000.

with the maturity close to the year you retire. This is a risk-free scenario only if you hold the bonds to maturity, and should be used in combination with stocks or mutual funds.

Zero-Coupon Bonds

These are interesting yet complex bonds that will pay you a set amount in the future in exchange for no interest payments while you own them. Basically they are U.S. Treasury securities stripped of the coupon. That means that you are getting only a promise to repay principal at a future date. The coupon part is removed, so you don't get any interest payment while you hold them. The agreement is that the prices of the bonds are heavily discounted in exchange for the lack of interest.

The complexity of zeros comes in the calculation of the discounts. The prices of the zeros are directly tied into current interest rates. Like other bonds, the longer the maturity, the greater the volatility. Zeros with thirty-year maturities can move up to 30% if interest rates move 1% in either direction. Again, the inverse relationship with interest rates is in force as well: If rates move down, you could see as much as a 30% gain in the principal value—or a loss if rates shoot up.

You can buy zeros directly through brokers—and pay a commission—or buy them packaged by a maturity date (from five to thirty years out) through American Century/Benham (800-345-2021) or Scudder Investments (800-225-2470). The mutual fund route is the most convenient since you get a diversified portfolios of zeros. Part of the strategy of zeros is to go long on maturities when rates are dropping and go short when rates are rising. You can lock in capital gains within an IRA if there are major moves in rates. It's unwise to speculate, but the important thing to remember is to preserve those gains by moving from portfolio to portfolio. The following table illustrates how zeros work:

ZERO-COUPON BONDS: HOW THEY WORK

Current Int. Rate (percent)	Desired Amount	Years to Maturity	You Pay Now
7	$100,000	10	$50,305
7	$100,000	15	$35,665
7	$100,000	20	$25,285
7	$250,000	10	$125,760
7	$250,000	15	$89,153
7	$250,000	20	$63,205

SOURCE: Shearson Lehman Hutton Zero Coupon Treasury Calculator

This table illustrates the discounted nature of zeros. The longer the maturity, the greater the discount. Although this is based on buying individual bonds with one lump sum, you can start with any amount if you invest through a mutual fund. If interest rates or the time you have until maturity changes, then the assumptions change. If you can project when you'll need the money, that's the best way to start. Then figure out how much you can commit to zeros, which should comprise no more than 15% of your portfolio if you have at least twenty years to save. If you have under fifteen years to invest, raise the percentage of bonds in your portfolio to 20%; under fifteen years, 25% to 30%.

One note: Few people know that EE savings bonds are really zeros in disguise. You can buy them at 50% discount of face amount, i.e., a $100 bond costs $50. Upon maturity—usually ten years or so, depending on the bond—you can cash the bond in for its full face amount. Savings bonds, however, are not the best investments for your late-start portfolio. While they still carry that government guarantee, you can do better in terms of yield elsewhere.

Zeros get even thornier at tax time. You pay tax on "imputed" interest—interest you would have received if the bonds had a coupon. So zeros are best held in an IRA, where the tax issue is not a problem.

Buying Municipal Bonds

Going from the muddled word of zeros to the straightforward world of municipal bonds is easy. Municipal bonds are federal tax-free instruments issued by state, county, and local agencies to finance things like roads, buildings, and other infrastructure. Depending on the health of the agency issuing them, these bonds are generally regarded as safe in the credit-risk department. Like corporate bonds, they are all rated for creditworthiness by Moody's and Standard & Poor's. The lower the letter in the alphabet—i.e., AAA or Aa—the better the credit risk. The capital letters mean a better rating; all capital As are best.

Here's the simple part: Don't buy individual munis unless (1) you are in the 28% tax bracket or above, or (2) you have at least $1 million to properly diversify among single bonds. The one exception is being in the higher tax bracket and investing through mutual funds. If you have a real need to reduce your taxable income, then you can incorporate munis into your portfolio, but they should be no more than 15% of your portfolio. Otherwise stick to corporate or treasury bonds or funds. Muni yields are discounted to reflect the tax-free nature of the yield. For example, a 3.25% tax-free return sounds pretty paltry. But that's 4.51% in the 28% tax bracket due to the fact that you get to keep more of the yield away from Uncle Sam. Always compare the tax-free yield with current taxable yields. You may find you'll get better yields in taxable vehicles.

Money Market Funds

These are among the simplest and highest-utility income vehicles. Nearly every major mutual fund group offers them and yields are highly competitive. The best-managed funds will waive management expenses to get your business. Don't buy them through banks, where they are called money market deposit accounts. Brokers also offer them, but nip yields by imposing 12 b-1 fees, where your yield is reduced to help the broker market the fund to others. They are typically lower yielding and will only allow three checks per month.

As part of your cash-management program, use money market accounts for money you'll need from month to month to pay bills. Managers invest money market funds in treasury bills and short-term corporate paper with maturities generally under one year. That's why the cost per share is fixed at $1. You can use money market funds for escrow accounts, short-term cash needs, and emergency funds. They are not good for long-term savings, as they track only short-term interest rates, which will put you behind the pace of inflation. For those in the 28% tax bracket and above, consider tax-free money market funds if the yields look good to you.

Building Your Income Portfolio

CASH-MANAGEMENT/EMERGENCY FUND

Fund	Type	Minimum Invest.	Phone (800)
Vanguard MMRP	MMF	$3,000	851-4999
Benham Prime	MMF	$2,500	345-2021
Strong MM	MMF	$1,000	368-3863
Calvert TFRes.	Tax-free	$2,000	368-2748
USAA TEMM	Tax-free	$3,000	382-8722

NOTE: these funds have consistently produced high yields as measured by *IBC's Money Fund Report.*

SHORT-TERM SAVINGS (UNDER FIVE YEARS)

Fund	Type	Phone (800)
Strong Short-Term	Corp.	368-1030
Vanguard STC	Corp.	662-7447
Sit U.S. Govt. Sec.	U.S. Govt.	332-5580

MID-TERM SAVINGS (FIVE YEARS OR MORE)

Fund	Type	Phone (800)
Vanguard FIG	GNMA	662-7447
T. Rowe Price TFHY	Tax-free	638-5660
Safeco High Yield	Corp.	426-6730
Lindner Dividend	High yield stocks	995-7777
Vanguard BITBM	Mixed	662-7447

Summary: Bonds Bolster Growth Vehicles

1. Know that bonds are used to provide diversification and some safety. They are not immune to market risk.

2. Diversify using government, zeros, or municipal bonds. Stagger maturities and reduce risk further through "laddering."

3. Although bonds complement stocks, they are better for short-term savings and for buffering risk if you have less than ten years to go before retirement.

4. Choose income mutual funds or money market funds that have professional management and are diversified.

CHAPTER 10

Seeking and Finding Balance

"If you dream it, it will wake others up at night."

Life is a ballet between what you need to sustain yourself and what life provides you to do it. The French have a wonderful phrase for this balanced existence: *paix et peu.* Literally, it means "peace and little." Generally it's taken to mean a peaceful life on a modest income with the emphasis on peace and life and not income.

Balance is often a matter of finding that reserve of energy in you and applying it at the right time. When I was studying Tai Chi and Qi Gong, two ancient Chinese arts of exercise and energy balancing, I discovered how difficult it is to find that balance. Tai Chi Master Shengli Wang was anxious to demonstrate this in one of the classes I was taking. Since I was one of the largest people in the room, I was the immovable object to be pushed off balance. I expected to be downed by a sophisticated Tai Chi throw like a thug in a Kung Fu movie. So I planted my feet and lowered my hips. I knew I would be tested and perhaps humiliated by a man half my size. Master Sheng didn't have to grab or throw me at all. I learned there really aren't any such throws in Tai Chi. All he did was tap my shoulder and I went flying! I didn't believe what I felt, so he did it again and I flew across the room again. He explained that he transmitted his *chi,* or life energy, into my body. The resulting jolt threw me off balance. This demonstration taught me that life energy could be directed, channeled to change one's direction in life.

Clearly the overriding theme of this book is seeking balance: balance in your personal life, your career, and your financial goals. If these three components are in conflict, you will not be able to approach your New Prosperity plan with any vigor. Life's unrelenting chaos doesn't give us much time to find that balance. And just when we get a chance to take a breather, we're assaulted with more bad news on Social Security, our jobs, or our environment. It's stressful just to think about it.

If we want to boost our sagging savings accounts in order to pay for this New Prosperity, we're presented with millions of temptations to spend more. A potent combination of ever-present advertising and easy credit makes it easy for us to obtain anything we want when we want it. No wonder a record 1.3 million Americans filed for personal bankruptcy in 1997, up nearly 20 percent from 1996.[1]

Imagine what most households could do with the average $7,000 in credit-card debt they hold if they invested that money instead.[2] At a modest 12% annual return, that money would compound into $28,000 in twelve years, $56,000 in eighteen years, and $112,000 in twenty-four years. And that's if you invested it fairly conservatively in an average stock mutual fund. You can't argue with arithmetic, although most of us fight it every day.

We're often taught that aging is a negative experience and that old age represents nothing but deterioration, poverty, and dependence. The rewarding part about aging, however, is that it also buys us time. Time to mend our ways. Time to grow our own prosperity, to find work we like, and to spend time and money on things that count.

I once sat next to Betty Friedan at a conference in New York in which she was given a Lifetime Achievement Award from the

American Society of Journalists and Authors. In addition to being one of the pioneers of the feminist movement, Betty has written extensively about the many benefits of aging, one of them being the acquisition of wisdom. She said she was flattered to be recognized as a writer after having been given every accolade under the sun for her work as a feminist leader. Sitting there next to greatness, I wanted to ask her something, but was totally intimidated and tongue-tied. What do you ask one of the most influential persons of the century? What question could I ask that she hadn't already been asked a million times before? Here I was, twenty years into my craft, having done thousands of interviews, and I froze up.

After the conference, I relayed my anguish to my wife and colleagues. Then I realized something. Betty Friedan's *life* was both question and answer. She asked questions and *life* responded. Isn't that something we should be doing every day? Just asking of life what we should be doing rather than following someone else's script? After all, advertisers try to make us doubt ourselves. Ironically, it makes us ask all the wrong questions. It doesn't matter if we're not beautiful, sexy, or rich enough. It doesn't matter if we have the newest car or the latest electronic devices or can easily lose a few more pounds. What matters is that we ask questions that pertain to *us*. You know who you are. Nobody can define who you are. Nobody can say how much money you should make and save or the manner in which you should do it. I believe this is what Thomas Jefferson meant when he referred to the "pursuit of happiness." He meant we have the right to be self-reliant in asking our own questions about our destiny.

So our personal ecology—our relationship with ourselves and the world—comes down to something hauntingly simple. Even if you don't know what you want to do with the rest of your life, you should have a good time asking the questions. The answers, which may not come with the next sunrise, will continue to intrigue you.

Summary: The New Prosperity Is Within Yourself

1. **Ask some critical questions about your work life. Are you doing what you want to do?**

2. Do you need new education or training to do different work? What does it entail? How much does it cost?

3. What are the important things that make life worth living? List all of the nonfinancial considerations that are important to you and include them in your New Prosperity plan.

4. Consider a balance to your plan. What adds or diminishes your life energy?

5. Start your plan. Enjoy.

NOTES

PREFACE

1. Henry David Thoreau, *Walden*, as quoted in *The Winged Life* by Robert Bly (HarperPerennial, 1987), p. 7.

CHAPTER 1. THE TRUTH ABOUT RETIREMENT, SOCIAL SECURITY, AND PENSIONS

1. Donald Bartlett and James Steele, *America: Who Stole the Dream?* (Andrews & McMeel, 1996), p. 214.
2. Concord Coalition, 1996 Annual Report.
3. Cato Institute, 1996 Annual Report.
4. Final Report, Bipartisan Commission on Entitlement Reform, 1995.
5. Telephone interview with Professor Guilarducci.
6. Social Security Trustees Report, 1996.
7. Reuters news service, January 8, 1998.

CHAPTER 2. YOUR NEW PROSPERITY GOALS

1. Retirement Confidence Survey 1996, Employee Benefit Research Institute, Washington, D.C.
2. Ibid.
3. "Rethinking Retirement," by Paula Mergenhagen, *American Demographics*, June 1994.
4. Ibid.

5. Ibid.
6. Ibid.
7. EBRI, above.

Chapter 3. Lifestyle Planning: Getting the Life You Want

1. Tad Crawford, *The Secret Life of Money* (Tarcher-Putnam, 1994), p. 61.
2. Jacob Needleman, *Money and the Meaning of Life* (Doubleday, 1991), p. 117.
3. Erik Erikson, *Childhood and Society* (Norton, 1978), p. 274.
4. Ibid., p. 275.
5. Ibid.
6. "The Soul of Money," a transcribed radio interview with Lynne Twist, New Dimensions Radio, 1997.
7. Telephone interview with Dottie Koontz, December 1996.
8. Michael Jacobson and Laurie Ann Mazur, *Marketing Madness: A Survival Guide for a Consumer Society* (Westview Press, 1995), p. 194.
9. ". . . and Deeper in Debt," *The Economist,* June 7, 1997.
10. *Marketing Madness*, p. 195.
11. A. C. Nielsen Company Survey, 1995.
12. "Why Millions Celebrate the TV-Turnoff Week," *San Diego Union-Tribune,* April 24, 1996.
13. Alan Thein Durning, *How Much Is Enough?* (Norton, 1992), p. 25.
14. John Kenneth Galbraith, *The Affluent Society* (Houghton-Mifflin, 1976), p. 169.

Chapter 4. Investing in Yourself

1. *Report 900*, U.S. Bureau of Labor Statistics, p. 7, 1996.
2. Ibid.
3. Ibid.
4. Richard Judy and Carol D'Amico, *Workforce 2020: Work and Workers in the 21st Century* (Hudson Institute, 1997), p. 78.
5. William Wolman and Anne Colamosca, *The Judas Economy* (Addison-Wesley, 1997), p. 206.
6. Press release, Challenger, Gray & Christmas, March 12, 1996.
7. Press release, TV-Free America, 1997.
8. Ibid.

Chapter 5. Getting Smart, Getting Savvy Fast

1. Ed Mrkvicka, *Your Bank Is Ripping You Off* (St. Martin's Griffin, 1997), p. 114.

2. Ibid., p. 113.

3. Consumer Federation of America study, 1997.

CHAPTER 9. ANCHORING YOUR PORTFOLIO: THE ROLE OF BONDS

1. The most current information on bonds is contained in *The Wall Street Journal* or the *Investors Business Daily*, or through the U.S. Treasury's website at http://www.ustreas.gov.

CHAPTER 10. SEEKING AND FINDING BALANCE

1. Reuters Business Wire, January 7, 1998.

2. Ibid.

RESOURCES

Books

Bartlett, Donald, and James Steele, *America: Who Stole the Dream?* (Andrews McMeel, 1996). A comprehensive look at what's wrong with our economy.

Burch, Mark, *Simplicity: Notes, Stories, and Exercises for Developing Unimaginable Wealth* (New Society Publishers, 1995). The genuine article on simplifying your lifestyle.

Crawford, Tad, *The Secret Life of Money: Teaching Tales of Spending, Receiving, Saving, and Owing* (Tarcher Putnam, 1994). An absolute gem on the meaning of money in all of its forms.

Dominguez, Joe, and Vicki Robin, *Your Money or Your Life: Transforming Your Relationship with Money and Achieving Financial Independence* (Penguin, 1993). The bestselling classic on becoming financially independent.

Durning, Alan, *How Much Is Enough? The Consumer Society and the Future of the Earth* (Worldwatch Institute, 1992). The downside of our consumer society and what you can do about it.

Hudson Institute, *Workforce 2020: Work and Workers in the 21st Century.* A leading think tank's incisive look at the future of employment in the United States.

Jacobson, Michael, and Laurie Ann Mazur, *Marketing Madness: A Survival Guide for a Consumer Society* (Westview Press, 1995). How advertising is hurting our culture. This book has no peer.

Jason, Julie, *You and Your 401(k): How to Manage Your 401(k) for Maximum Returns* (Fireside, 1996). One of the most useful, down-to-earth books on this complex subject.

Mrkvicka, Ed, *Your Bank Is Ripping You Off* (St. Martin's Griffin, 1997). A former bank president's inside look at saving big on mortgages and other installment loans.

Orman, Suze, *The Nine Steps to Financial Freedom: Practical and Spiritual Steps So You Can Stop Worrying* (Crown, 1997). An excellent guide to mastering the practical and spiritual aspects of money.

United Seniors Health Cooperative, *Long-Term Care Planning: A Dollars and Sense Guide*. A fine primer on a complex subject. Order directly from USHC, 1331 H St. NW, Suite 500, Washington, DC 20005, 202-393-6222.

Warner, Ralph, *Get a Life: You Don't Need a Million to Retire Well* (Nolo Press, 1996). A simple guide to retirement by one of the leading self-help publishers.

MAGAZINES AND NEWSLETTERS

Barron's, Business Week, Forbes, Smart Money, Worth.

Better Investing, 248-583-6242, 711 W. Thirteen-Mile Rd., Madison Heights, MI 48071. A superb resource for do-it-yourself stock investors.

Dow Theory Forecasts, 212-931-6480.

The Moneypaper, 1010 Mamaroneck Ave., Mamaroneck, NY 10543. A newsletter that not only provides lists of stock dividend reinvestment plans, but advice to go along with them.

NAIC Investors Advisory Service, 810/583-NAIC.

No-Load Stock Insider, 219-852-3230, 7412 Calumet Ave., Suite 200, Hammond, IN 46324-2692. The leading resource on money-saving direct-purchase and dividend-revinvestment stock plans.

Simple Living Journal, 206-464-4800 (www.simpleliving.com). Although a bit too commercial for my tastes, still a useful resource for books and articles on voluntary simplicity.

Value Line, found in the library.

Your Money, 847-763-9200. one of the most informative and down-to-earth personal finance magazines.

SERVICES (PHONE NUMBERS AND WEBSITES)

American Institute of Certified Public Accountants, 800-862-4272. A referral service that will provide names of accountants with training in financial planning in your area.

American Society of CLU and ChFC, 888-243-2258. This service will locate a qualified insurance agent/financial adviser near you.

Bankcard Holders of America, 540-389-5445. This group will provide lists of no/low-fee credit cards.

Bureau of Public Debt, 304-480-6112 (www.ustreas.gov). A key source for information on savings and Treasury bonds.

Consumer Credit Counseling Service, 800-388-2227 (www.nfcc .org). Deep in debt and having trouble making payments? This nonprofit service will locate a counseling center near you.

Debtors Anonymous, 212-642-8220. A support group that will help you develop an action plan to pare down your debts.

Debt Counselors of America, 800-680-3328 (www.dca.org). Another service designed to help you make repayment plans on large debts.

Direct Stock Purchase Plan Clearinghouse, 800-774-4117. A service that links you to commission-free direct-stock purchase plans of major corporations.

Gamblers Anonymous, 800-426-2537. A support group for compulsive gamblers.

Good Advice Press, 914-758-1400, PO Box 78, Elizaville, NY 12523 (investinu@ulster.net). An excellent resource for publications and software on debt and mortgage reduction strategies.

Institute of Certified Financial Planners, 800-438-7526, 800-438-9968 TTY. This group will provide a list of three planners in your area and a brochure on selecting a planner.

International Association for Financial Planning, 800-945-IAFP. A trade group that will provide referrals to financial planners near you.

National Association of Investors Corporation, 248-583-6242, 711 W. Thirteen-Mile Rd., Madison Heights, MI 48071 (www.better-investing.org). This nonprofit group provides help in setting up stock investment clubs.

National Association of Personal Financial Advisers, 800-FEE-ONLY. This group will provide referrals to noncommissioned financial planners.

National Association of Securities Dealers, 800-289-9999. A disclosure service that will tell you if a particular broker-dealer has had any disciplinary history.

National Credit Counseling Service, 800-955-0412 (www.nccs .org). Additional debt counseling help.

Securities and Exchange Commission, 800-732-0330. The federal agency will tell you if a registered investment adviser has been fined, reprimanded or suspended.

Social Security Administration, 800-772-1213 (www.ssa.gov). A good place to start to estimate your Social Security benefits. Ask for the PEBES form.

PERSONAL FINANCE/INVESTING WEBSITES

All of these Internet websites will either help you save, invest or buy products at a discount. All of the information is free, however, you'll need a computer, modem, and phone line to access. (Note: all websites have prefix: http://)

Government-Sponsored Sites

Bureau of Labor Statistics (www.bls.gov) Want to know if your salary is keeping up with inflation? How about the fastest-growing industries? A rich source of employment information.

Census Bureau (www.census.gov) All the numbers on population and people.

Consumer Information Center (www.pueblo.gsa.gov) A cornucopia of free government information on everything from pensions to Social Security.

EDGAR/SEC filings See Securities and Exchange Commission.

General Accounting Office (www.gao.gov) Congress's watchdog agency probes nearly every kind of government activity. You can search for GAO reports and order them online.

Internal Revenue Service (www.irs.ustreas.gov) The mother lode of tax forms and publications.

Library of Congress (lcweb.loc.gov) A one-stop site for government information and other federal websites. You can also check for nearly any book in print.

National Association of Securities Dealers (www.nasdr.com) This quasi-government agency partially regulates securities dealers. You can check the background on your broker, learn about securities fraud and warnings from the National Fraud Information Center, or obtain basic rules governing stockbrokers.

Pension Benefit Guaranty Agency (www.pbgc.gov) The place to start for anything concerning defined-benefit pension plans or locating lost defined-benefit pensions.

Securities and Exchange Commission (www.sec.gov) The main entry point to the SEC's EDGAR database of filings by public companies. An invaluable resource for stock investors. Also check out www.edgar.stern.nyu.edu/mutual.html for SEC filings by mutual funds. EDGAR Online: 203-834-6282.

Social Security Administration (www.ssa.gov) One of the most popular government sites on the Internet. Contains every Social Security publication and answers to common Social Security questions.

U.S. Department of Labor, Pension and Welfare Benefits Administration (www.dol.gov/dol/pwba) A useful source for publications on how to monitor your pension plan's investments from the agency that polices fund managers.

U.S. Department of the Treasury (www.ustreas.gov) An indispensable source for everything concerning Treasury and savings bonds.

U.S. House of Representatives (www.house.gov) A useful site for member information, committee assignments, and e-mail addresses.

U.S. Senate (www.senate.gov) Ditto for the Senate.

White House (www.whitehouse.gov) Search for the president's latest speeches and press releases and general information on the office of the president.

Commercial Sites

These sites essentially prompt you to buy the sponsor's product or services, but contain a number of useful pieces of information and software. You are under no obligation to purchase their wares, however.

Bank Rate Monitor (www.bankrate.com) A primary source for the best rates on certificates of deposit, credit cards, and mortgages nationwide.

Scott Burns (www.scottburns.com) Some useful personal finance columns from the syndicated writer.

Consumer Law Page (www.consumerlawpage.com) Although sponsored by the Alexander Law Firm, a treasure trove of information on consumer law, class-action suits, and consumer complaints.

Deloitte & Touche (www.dtonline.com) A handy resource on taxes, financial planning, and retirement issues.

Fidelity Mutual Funds (www.fid-inv.com) While this is a big billboard for hundreds of Fidelity products, check out their "Thinkware" retirement planning software.

Finance Center/SmartCalc (www.financenter.com) Easily one of the most practical financial calculators on the Internet. You can estimate everything from car payments to retirement savings.

Get Smart (www.getsmart.com) Credit card information.

HSH (www.hsh.com) The best mortgage rates in the United States.

Huntington (www.huntington.com) This bank offers very basic financial information and advice.

Ibbotson (www.ibbotson.com) Historical information on investments.

IBC Financial Data (www.ibcdata.com) The first place to check for the best returns on money market mutual funds and bond funds.

Insurance Corner (www.insurancecorner.com) A master site for consumer information on insurance agents and news.

Intuit (www.intuit.com) From the makers of Quicken and Turbo-Tax, this site features software and advice. Also see "www .quicken.com" for useful financial calculators.

Invest-o-rama (www.investorama.com) Provides links to more than 2,000 investment-related sites.

Lawresearch (www.lawresearch.com) Law firm websites organized by specialty and state.

Lifenet (www.lifenet.com) Mortgage calculators and worksheets.

Morningstar (www.morningstar.net) One of the most engaging and useful sites on the web. Includes profiles of stocks and mutual funds. One of the best features is an online portfolio monitoring program that will automatically store and update values on all of your stock and bond holdings.

Mortgage Maze (www.maze.com) Mortgage qualifying calculator and credit information (order credit reports online).

Nest Egg (www.nestegg.iddis.com) A large site sponsored by *Investment Dealer Digest*, it features mutual funds, stocks, a retirement calculator, and financial news and articles.

Netstock Direct (www.netstockdirect.com) A daily listing of direct-stock purchase plans.

Networth (www.networth.galt.com) Fund information and portfolio tracking program.

PCFN (www.pcfn.com) Run by a securities brokerage. A good source for stock quotes, charts, research, and news from Reuters, Business Wire, and PR News—all of which is searchable. You can even build portfolios online.

T. Rowe Price (www.troweprice.com) The best retirement planning software on the Internet.

Quicken (networth.quicken.com) An omnibus site that allows you to track ten portfolios, obtain stock quotes, track the top-performing mutual funds, and much more. See Intuit.

Quote.com (Quote.com) Electronic mail stock-quote and alert service.

RAM Research (www.ramresearch.com) A primary source to find the best deals on any type of credit card.

Research Magazine (www.researchmag.com) Research on stocks and financial advice.

Charles Schwab (www.schwab.com) An omnibus site that includes everything from college savings calculators to free charting of stocks. Delayed stock quotes also available.

Strong Funds (www.strong-funds.com) Provides basic investment/retirement information in its education section.

Vanguard (www.vanguard.com) Check out their retirement center and compounding computer.

Waddell (www.waddell.com) Features a retirement calculator and basic investment information.

Webfinance (www.webfinance.net) A master site that links you to other commercial sites.

Information Services/Search Engines/Hybrids
These services are pure information retrievers, pulling all sorts of things from cyberspace, phone books, and beyond.

AltaVista (www.altavista.digital.com) One of the most comphrehensive search engines available.

Excite (www.excite.com) A search engine hybrid that offers yellow page listings, stock quotes, maps, newsgroups, and e-mail lookups. Not as good as Infoseek or AltaVista, though.

Hoover's Online (www.hoovers.com) Company profiles and links to other sites. Also available on America Online.

Infoseek (www.infoseek.com) A diverse hybrid that combines indexing, search engines, and other gateways to yellow pages and e-mail lookups. You can also put an Infoseek "button" on your browser to avoid going directly to their website.

Lycos (www.lycos.com) Your basic search engine.

Mercury Mail (www.merc.com) Will automatically send "closing bell" stock prices and company news as well as headlines from Reuter's News Service.

Newslink (www.newslink.org) Links to more than 3,000 publication-sponsored sites.

Pointcast Network (pointcast.com) One of the leading "push" technology providers, Pointcast will deliver stock quotes, industry/company news, and a variety of other items from CNN and *The Wall Street Journal* directly onto your computer screen.

Pointcom (www.pointcom.com) A search engine/index run by Lycos but based more on Yahoo.

QuikPages (www.quikpage.com) A national directory of business websites.

SavvySearch (www.cs.colostate.edu/~dreiling/smartform.html) A multi-site search engine that searches several search engines at once, although not very well.

Yahoo (www.yahoo.com) Relying more on lists of indexes, Yahoo is all things to all people in cyberspace.

Media Sites

Although offering limited information, these sites are good places for background information on nearly any financial topic.

Barron's Online (www.barrons.com) The weekly Dow Jones investment magazine features stock and fund information.

Bloomberg Business News (www.bloomberg.com) News on companies and portfolio management software.

Business Wire (www.businesswire.com) Company press releases and news.

CNN (www.cnn.com) Headlines from the Cable News Networkand CNN's "fn" financial news channel.

MSNBC (www.msnbc.com) Briefs from the cable network's news coverage also includes some NBC News items.

The New York Times (www.nytimes.com) Lead stories from the national newspaper. Also on American Online.

Pathfinder (www.pathfinder.com) Time-Warner's enormous master site features *Fortune*, *Money*, and the rest of the huge stable of Time-Warner publications and entertainment media.

Reuter's News Service (www.reuters.com) Hot stories from the Reuter's wire service.

USA Today (www.usatoday.com) A quirky but searchable site.

The Wall Street Journal (www.wsj.com) An abbreviated version of the financial newspaper. For the full, searchable version, you pay a subscription fee.

The Washington Post (www.washingtonpost.com) A generous site that includes archived stories from the *Post*'s fine columnists, including Jane Bryant Quinn. Its most valuable feature, however, is the ability to search the Associated Press news wires.

Worth Magazine (www.worth.com) The website is actually better than the magazine, which is owned by Fidelity Investments. Features include "Ask Peter Lynch," message boards, and useful financial links.

Miscellaneous Consumer/Shopping (Includes Nonprofit and Trade Groups)
These sites will help you save money on any number of consumer products.

Autosite (www.autosite.com) A vehicle pricing and buying service.

Carsmart (www.carsmart.com) Vehicle-pricing service with links to dealers and manufacturers featuring invoice prices.

CCSNY (www.ccsny.org/weblinks) Essential links to consumer groups, credit information, and government information.

Consumers Digest (www.consumersdigest.com) Ratings and information on a wide range of consumer products.

Consumer Guide (www.cg.gte.net) Brief reviews of a wide range of consumer products from autos to household goods.

Consumer World (www.consumerworld.org) If you go no other place on the web for consumer information, try this site first. Its 1,500 links are incomparable, everything from the best deals in credit cards to a "private eye" section for locating people, products, and information.

Equifax (www.equifax.com) Information on credit reports.

Essential Information (www.esssential.org) The master site that will link you to most of the Nader-founded consumer groups, including the Center for Auto Safety, Center for Insurance Research, Center for Science in the Public Interest, Center for Public Integrity, Coalition for Consumer Health and Safety, and Public Citizen.

Experian (www.experian.com) Information from the credit-bureau service formerly called TRW.

GTE Superpages (www.gte.net) A master site for searches of phone books, yellow pages, classified ads, employment ads, and business websites.

HOME (www.hometips.com) Sponsored by *Home* Magazine, a treasure trove of buying advice on hundreds of home-related products.

Investment Company Institute (www.ici.org) Sponsored by the trade group for the mutual fund industry, this site features updated news on legislation and subjects impacting investors.

Kelley Blue Book (www.kbb.com) The premier source for vehicle prices (used and new) anywhere.

Mutual Fund Education Alliance (www.mfea.com) The mutual fund trade group features a retirement worksheet.

Mutual Funds Interactive (www.fundsinteractive.com) News and discussion on mutual fund topics.

National Association of Enrolled Agents (www.naea.org) The latest tax news and information on income taxes and filing tips.

Parent Soup (www.parentsoup.com) Reviews of baby products, videos, and software.

PC World (www.pcworld.com) Reviews of computers and peripherals.

Popular Mechanics (www.popularmechanics.com) Reviews on vehicles and electronics and articles on home-improvement topics.

Product Reviews (www.productreviewnet.com) Reviews on thousands of appliances, vehicles, computers, and health and beauty items.

INDEX